THERE'S ALWAYS A WAY

By Kevin Saunders
and Bob Darden

WRS
PUBLISHING

A Division of WRS Group, Inc.
Waco, Texas

First published in the United States of America in 1993 by WRS Publishing, A Division of WRS Group, Inc., 701 N. New Road, Waco, Texas 76710.
Book design by Kenneth Turbeville
Jacket design by Talmage Minter
Front cover photo by George Gongora
Back cover photos by Dan Brock

10 9 8 7 6 5 4 3 2 1

Library of Congress Cataloging-in-Publication Data

Saunders, Kevin, 1955-
   There's always a way / by Kevin Saunders and Bob Darden.
     p. cm.
   ISBN 1-56796-018-9 : $12.95
   1. Saunders, Kevin, 1955—Health. 2. Paraplegics—United States—
Biography. I. Darden, Bob, 1954-   . II. Title.
RC406.P3S28 1993
362.4'3'092—dc20
   [B]   93-27549
                                                       CIP

Dedication

To the late John Diamantakiou,

the driving force in Senator Dole's

office in securing Kevin's

appointment, as the first disabled

person, to the President's Council

on Physical Fitness and Sports.

Foreword

One of the more enjoyable experiences that face a president of the United States is meeting the people who come to the Oval Office to be recognized for some achievement. During my administration, one of those people was Kevin Saunders.

I had heard of Kevin long before I actually met him, and knew that his story was almost unbelievable. I knew he had survived a dreadful grain-elevator explosion in Texas, was aware that he had had to overcome incredible physical and personal obstacles, and I knew he had become—through the sheer force of his will—the world's greatest wheelchair athlete and an eloquent spokesman for the rights of the physically challenged.

Kevin and I have met several times since that day in the Oval Office. Each time, I'm more impressed with his perseverance and courage. What fuels my admiration is the knowledge that the most frightening moments of my life—and I was shot down twice in World War II—are not equal to what Kevin experiences on a regular basis.

It is my hope that the Americans with Disabilities Act, which, I am proud to say, was passed during my term as president, will enable others like Kevin Saunders, who daily face the challenges of living in a world designed for able-bodied people, to be more fully integrated into every facet of American life.

There's Always a Way is the story of how Kevin responded to an almost overwhelming situation, changing himself and his life in the process. I hope you will find it inspiring and uplifting.

George Bush
Houston, Texas
Spring 1993

Chapter 1

April 7, 1981, the day everything changed, dawned clear and bright in Corpus Christi, Texas.

Recently graduated from Kansas State University, Kevin Saunders and his wife Brenda[1] were still living in their upstairs apartment at 1310 Sixth Street, making plans to move to their new house at 4209 Live Oak. They'd only been married several months, so they still considered themselves newlyweds. Oh, they fought an awful lot—Kevin always said that she had a hair-trigger temper—but making up afterwards was always so very nice.

Kevin let Brenda sleep late that day. He dressed quietly for his job as a federal grain inspector, had a quick breakfast, and bounded down the stairs to his car.

Everything seemed perfectly normal.

"I'll never forget walking down to get in my car to go to work that day," Kevin recalled. "We lived about six or seven miles from the elevator. To get to the elevator, I drove down Ocean Drive, took Highway 37 north toward San Antonio, then on to the Port of Corpus Christi Public Elevator. I'll never forget that ride, either.

"It was just another day; I had no qualms about going to the elevator, despite its problems with grain dust or its violations of government regulations."

He was at that particular elevator that day to check on dust collection. Grain dust is highly flammable. In high concentrations in a confined space—like a silo—it can also be highly explosive. Kevin had checked the elevator out before and found it to be below operating standards. But the elevator personnel seemed indifferent.

The Port of Corpus Christi Public Elevator is on Navigation Boulevard on the north side of the Port of Corpus Christi ship channel. It is a gigantic, sprawling complex. From a distance, the containment silos look like a pack of giant cigarettes standing straight up.

The complex was built about 1953. It was, and is, one of the largest such complexes in the world. At peak capacity, the elevator's silos can hold about 6.5 million bushels of grain. Its one previous major explosion had occurred in 1968. After safety regulations tightened in the 1970s, grain dust collectors were added in 1980 at a cost of $3.5 million.

Kevin was part of a regular working crew of seven inspectors making routine Department of Agriculture inspections at the elevator.

Against the white walls of the Public Grain Elevator, he and all of the more than fifty people who were on the scene that day looked like ants as they scurried in and out of the doors at ground level. Kevin was making his rounds at the elevator that day, looking for problems or potentially dangerous situations—anything that didn't look right. After a while, he went to the government weights lab to do the paperwork on the inventory. It was such a slow day, he even considered leaving early.

"About 3:10 p.m., I heard something like a sonic boom, followed by a slow rumbling sound, like railroad cars bumping together. I said, 'What the hell's going on?'

"I felt the rumbling even in the lab. It started kinda slow, then grew in intensity. Suddenly, the ground itself was going up and down one to two feet. There was a popping and crackling that was so loud it seemed like it was gonna split my head open. I shot up from my desk, ready to run for the street.

"Then the explosions started."

Kevin and his supervisor Albert Tripp, inside the small metal laboratory, didn't see what happened next, but W.M. Jenkins, labor foreman for the elevator, did.

"There was a rumbling like thunder. Then boom! There it was," Jenkins told the *Corpus Christi Caller-Times*.

The initial explosions blew giant chunks of concrete, some weighing a ton or more, hundreds of yards from the silos. Eye-witnesses like Jenkins said it seemed as if the complex were being hit by rockets, or that rockets were being shot from inside the complex.

The explosions were heard—and some say felt—by residents living four and five miles away.

"Nobody had time to scream," one observer said. "They were just scattering in every direction."

"Fire came out of the windows and doors and everything started cracking up," Felix Escobar, an employee at the Centex cement plant one-half mile east of the main elevator building, told the *Caller-Times*.

John Van Meter, a contractor at the Champlin Oil Refinery, one mile away on the other side of the ship channel, said "All of a sudden, a huge ball of fire came out of one side of the [main] building, scattering pieces of stuff all over the place. It looked like a huge sledgehammer had hit it and taken off the tops of about ten silos. People were running around going nuts, and it looked like cement was falling."

The nightmarish scene on the grounds of the Public Elevator reminded some survivors of saturation bombing raids during World War II. Each of the five subsequent explosions was followed by a deadly rain of concrete. The parking lots and pavement walkways surrounding the elevator were littered with massive amounts of concrete, and long rods of reinforcing steel rebarb twisted in grotesque shapes.

Kevin and Albert were four hundred feet from the initial explosion site in A-House Silo, in the USDA-FRIS weights lab. The full force of the sixth, final, and largest explosion was channeled towards the flimsy sheet-metal structure called "C-House" at a rate of fifteen hundred feet per second.

"At that second, all hell broke loose," Kevin said. "I took it right in the face when it blew the window out. Albert hit the floor, but that didn't save him. One guy started to go out the door and was blown into a chain-link fence one hundred feet from the lab. He got hurt pretty bad—but he lived. Maybe that fence saved his life.

"The whole lab was reduced to rubble—it was completely destroyed except for the concrete foundation. The building was gone, just gone.

"In the heartbeat before the blast hit us, I remember looking over at Albert Tripp. I saw the look of death and desperation on his face. We all knew exactly what it was— a grain elevator explosion! We'd never seen one before, but we'd been schooled on them with slide presentations. Grain-dust explosions were the big thing in working with the Federal Inspection Service. I *knew* what kind of explosions grain dust could cause.

"The force that hit me was incredible; I'd never felt anything like it. It was like a giant fly swatter, swatting you. Few people get a chance to feel something like that— and live. Something hit me and took control of my whole body. I felt the whole window and wall explode in my face. The impact carried me and what was left of the room up through the roof and out on to the parking lot.

"I just had to ride it out. I guess my last thought was that I didn't expect to live."

Kevin remembered nothing else for several days.

He was blown three hundred feet through the roof into the air, over a two-story building and onto the elevator parking lot, just a few feet from the ship channel.

Following the final explosion, an eerie silence settled over the compound. For a brief moment, some survivors say, nothing stirred, not even flames. It was as if the entire scene had been captured in a still photograph.

Then, just as suddenly, the silence was gone, replaced by the screams of the injured, the wail of sirens, and the ferocious roar of the fire, which was feeding on millions of bushels of dry, crackling grain. Coughing, screaming, crying, cursing, the surviving elevator operators and federal inspectors staggered from the burning buildings.

Within minutes, ambulances, firetrucks, and media crews converged on the scene.

Among the many accounts of the next few hours, none are more evocative than the report filed by Steve Anton and Bruce Millar, staff writers of the *Corpus Christi Caller-Times:*

"The blood and the suffering were incomprehensible.

"Twisted and torn bodies squirmed unattended on concrete pavement. A few cried. Others were unconscious.

"Thick smoke billowed from several grain silos as the first fire trucks arrived at the scene.

"Inside the gates of the Corpus Christi Public Elevator, bodies were scattered everywhere. When it looked as if all the injured had been accounted for, more bodies were found under the massive debris.

"Frantic, confused workmen darted among their fellow employees not knowing whom to help first. A single ambulance had arrived, and the two attendants ran from one body to the next.

"One man grabbed an ambulance attendant by the arm and led him to an injured friend. Then he saw another injured man and pulled the attendant in that direction.

"A parking lot next to the silos looked like a battlefield. Small pools of blood formed beneath many of the injured while teams of workmen scurried to find makeshift splints and stretchers. They used blown-out doors and seat cushions and scraps of lumber to carry the victims to the ambulance and several private vehicles."

Steve and Bruce stood trembling as the horrific scenes of human despair and agony boiled around them. They saw men tumbling from doors and windows of the silos, their skin smoldering and emitting the pungent, sickening odor of burned flesh. Another man staggered by them, his clothes burned away, his blackened and hissing skin peeling off in bloody globs.

Ambulances had to pick through the debris. One ten-foot fist of concrete, at least two feet thick, had cut a two-foot-deep groove through Navigation Boulevard before imbedding itself in the pavement more than 300 feet away from the elevator.

Rescue helicopters swirled just above the spray in the ship channel, scanning the water for survivors—or bodies. Later in the day, other helicopters landed firefighters and engineers atop adjacent silos to cut burning conveyor belts that were continuing to spread the fire.

Fireballs spewed from the top of the burning elevator for more than an hour, igniting grass fires four hundred yards away.

Firefighting crews were forced to battle blazes in six of the giant concrete grain silos. Ultimately, some burned for several days as ladder crews were unable to reach pockets of smoldering grain. Towering clouds of black smoke rising from the wreckage could be seen from Corpus Christi six miles away.

Although ambulances screamed in from Corpus Christi and surrounding communities, the crush of bodies proved to be overwhelming. One ambulance left with seven injured people crammed in the back.

Corpus Christi Channel 6 captured particularly graphic video footage of the fire and its bloody aftermath. In one interview, harried Port of Corpus Christi spokesman Don Rodman told the audience that the grain dust collectors had been placed in the elevator primarily for environmental control reasons, "... and only secondarily for safety considerations."

The injured and burned were taken to the east side of the elevator. One of those injured was Kevin Saunders.

He was found, bent over, his face on his chest, a big knot on his back, blood coming out of his ears, nose and mouth, by two friends, Mark Lyum and Butch Anderson. Along with some of Kevin's other co-workers, they had been away from the elevator and were on their way back when they saw the explosion. The parking lot was already filled with bodies.

Mark was the first one to come upon Kevin's broken body, followed by Ed Loosemore. Both men thought that there was no way Kevin was going to survive.

Ed Loosemore was a safety inspector at Coast States Refinery and an officer with Refinery Terminal Fire Co. The company was composed of part-time firefighters drawn from the various refineries along the ship channel. Loosemore, like the others, was on call that afternoon.

He was at Coastal States when the explosion occurred, which is directly across the channel from the Public Silo.

He could see it, feel it and hear it. As the crow flies it's probably a mile, two miles away.

Loosemoore's pager went off, telling him what he already knew—that there was an emergency. So he and three other men hurried to the RTFC, which was only about two minutes away from Coastal States, for firetruck pickups. The wind was blowing out of the east and as they approached the elevator from the west side, for the last quarter-mile, they had to drive very slowly through the smoke.

Since other pumper trucks were already at work battling the blaze when they arrived, Loosemore and his crew were told to assist in search and rescue efforts on the grounds.

"Kevin was either the second or third person we found," Ed said. "We helped the city ambulance people move them to an emergency place in the parking lot where the paramedics were.

"I thought Kevin was dead. There was no life, no movement. I thought, 'There is no way this guy will make it.' Somebody told me where he had been before the explosion. When I thought about how far that was from where we found him I said, 'There is no way this guy is going to live.'"

Over the course of the afternoon, Loosemore and his team pulled six people out of the rubble. The death toll mounted hourly until nine were reported dead. Another twenty-nine were injured and admitted to Corpus Christi hospitals.

Ed's group helped to put out fires through several nights while still working their regular jobs during the day.

At one point, a helicopter was brought in to search for the last missing person—a security guard. Loosemoore was filming the helicopter landing when he and his co-workers saw something out in the channel. "We thought it was a bale of cotton or a bale of hay at first. We got closer and saw it was a body. When a boat came out and picked him up, they found that he still had on the uniform pants—so they knew it was the security guard."

What had happened? What had caused the death of ten people and injured so many more? Unfortunately, grain-elevator explosions have been around almost as long as there have been grain elevators. Since the turn of the century, more than five hundred people have died in the more than one thousand grain-elevator explosions that have occurred across the United States. The worst one in the twentieth century occurred December 22, 1977, in Westwego, Louisiana, where thirty-six people died at the Continental Grain Co. complex. Two other explosions within a week of the Louisiana blast killed an additional twenty people in Texas and Mississippi.

Strangely enough, on the same day of the Corpus Christi disaster, another explosion ripped through the Bellwood Farmer Co-op elevator in Bellwood, Nebraska, killing one man and critically injuring two others.

In most cases, grain dust explodes because it's under compression and a spark of some kind ignites it. Too much grain dust creates pressure that must be relieved. The Environmental Protection Agency ultimately blamed a buildup of grain dust for the Corpus Christi explosions.

There would be multiple lawsuits and a generation of legal finger-pointing, as virtually every concerned party tried to find someone to blame—and bill. But the generally accepted cause is that someone on top of one of the silos opened a can of phostoxin that, for some reason, produced a spark that set off the explosion. Investigators found unusually heavy deposits of grain dust in the damaged silos. That volume of grain dust compressed so tightly has the potential to create an enormously destructive organic bomb.

One final chapter to the disaster: a skinny, German Shepherd-mix puppy named Smiley had been adopted by the Public Grain Elevator employees in the months before the disaster. The day of the explosion, security guard Gilbert Garcia made his usual rounds, closely followed by his faithful shadow, Smiley. The blast blew them both out into the ship channel. The body of the nineteen-year-old Garcia, who had only been on the job five weeks, was found five days later by Loosemore.

But Smiley returned several days later, a little lame in the hind legs, but apparently intact. His whereabouts up to that time remain a mystery. In the weeks following the explosion, the dog still bolted at the slightest rumbling sound or machine backfire.

Even so, Smiley was one of the lucky ones. He went on to live a pampered life as the "good-luck" charm of the elevator employees.

But for Kevin Saunders, the nightmare had only just begun.

[1]Not her real name.

Chapter 2

Kevin Vaughn Saunders' grandfathers were farmers and Kevin was a farmer's son. Born on December 8, 1955 in Downs, Kansas, he was the third and final son of Donald and Freda Saunders. Kevin was something of a surprise. His older brothers, Gerald and Duane, were born February 25, 1935, and December 17, 1939, respectively. Freda Saunders was forty-one when Kevin was born; Donald was forty-five. Older brother Gerald graduated from Emporia State University in Emporia, Kansas, when Kevin was six months old.

Kevin was born into an idyllic *Wizard of Oz*-like setting—if the definition of "idyllic" includes dawn to dusk hard work, rolling hills of wheat that extend to every horizon, and winters that arrive early and stay late. The Saunders' farm was located in north central Kansas, thirteen miles from the geographical center of the United States, and seven miles north of Downs in Smith County.

There are few trees in this part of Kansas, save for along the roads and in Downs itself, a pleasant little town of about fifteen hundred when Kevin was growing up. It was, and is, a nice place to raise kids.

Like his German-born father, Donald Saunders grew wheat, grain sorghum, and alfalfa and raised cattle. For many years, he expected at least one of his sons to follow him on the land. By the time Kevin arrived, he was his father's last hope.

"It was a surprise having a baby that late, but it wasn't difficult," Freda recalled. "We had more time by then; we did a lot more with Kevin than we did with the older boys. We didn't have time when we were first starting this farm. Kevin was six months old when my oldest boy got married. When we'd go down to Kansas State to see

Duane play baseball, Kevin was like their mascot. They had a lot of fun with him."

Not surprisingly, little Kevin was treated more like a grandchild than a child, a precocious red-head given the run of the 240-acre farm, a posse of noisy, barking dogs forever in tow.

Kevin remembers usually being alone. The remoteness of the farm meant that there weren't any other kids to play with. His mother said that whenever company came, Kevin would want to entertain them and be the center of attention.

Gerald remembers that when he was young, he and his family would go to Downs to visit, and when they would get ready to go, none of the kids (Gerald's oldest son was about a year younger than Kevin) would be around! Kevin had taken them out into the wheat fields— they had run off so they wouldn't have to leave. "Kevin was lonely out on the farm and he was always wanting them to stay. He'd do anything to keep those kids from leaving."

Kevin was more lively, more active than her other boys— always wanting to do something, always talking, always wanting to be the center of attention.

Duane believes that Kevin's talkative, outgoing nature is an inheritance from their father Donald, who is now universally called Grandpa Saunders. Grandpa Saunders always adds a little bit to the story, just like Kevin does.

But all three boys agree that their father was the dominant personality force in their lives. Although he never attended school past the eighth grade, Donald Saunders was a successful farmer and nobody's fool. And none of his sons dared cross him.

"My father was a farmer, through and through," Gerald said. "He expected the corn rows to be straight. He was a hard worker and honest."

Donald Saunders instilled in his boys the importance of hard work as the means of getting what they wanted in life. His belief in being self-sufficient meant that they learned early not to expect others to provide for them. Freda Saunders feels this is why her three sons became such overachievers.

Living on a farm, where there was not a lot of money, all three boys had to work for spending money and take jobs early. By age fifteen Kevin went south to harvest with his second-cousin John Muck who had two combines. They traveled all the way to southern Kansas, Oklahoma, and Texas. And it was hard work, especially as it was in addition to the odd-jobs that needed to be done around the farm. That work ethic stayed with the boys throughout their adult lives, and according to Freda, attributed to their success later in life more than anything else.

"I think I spent every summer from ages fifteen to eighteen traveling with the harvest," Kevin said. "Each year we'd end up down in Oklahoma, working all day from dawn to midnight in that red dirt. Every time we took a shower it looked like blood going down the drain.

"My father expected a lot out of us, but never made us feel like we were failures," Gerald said. "Sometimes that's the case: Children feel that they can't live up to their parents expectations. We had to work hard to achieve his praise, but it would come—in time. So I think that was probably a key, that he left us with the idea that we could achieve; that we were winners, not failures."

"Winners" hardly describes the level of success the three Saunders boys ultimately achieved. Gerald became a successful certified public accountant and established Saunders & Co., P.A. in Simpsonville, South Carolina, a top public accounting firm in that part of the state and northern Georgia.

Duane graduated from the Mayo Clinic in physical therapy, and went on to establish a company specializing in industrial education an consultation. He is the part-owner of two physical therapy clinics, and has published textbooks and other instructional materials that are highly regarded in his field, particularly in the topic of back injury prevention.

"I think his parents had a lot to do with their childrens'

success," Jack Myers said. "They were from the old school. They made their children work, but they rewarded them for it. All three of them come from a good, strong background."

Whatever drove Gerald, Duane, and Kevin, all three Saunders boys did well in school and participated in high school athletics. Each of the three were elected president of the local Future Farmers of America chapter—in fact, Kevin was elected president twice! Kevin was also in 4-H (Home, Health, Heart and Hands) and had three champion bulls.

But none of the three showed an enduring interest in being a farmer.

"There was, to a certain extent, some pressure to stay and take over the farm," Gerald said. "All three of us probably would liked to have seen one or the other of us want to do it, but none of us wanted to, and none of us were made to feel like we needed to be afraid to pursue our own goals or be tied down by the fact that the farm had been in the family for several generations.

"The wind was what determined it for me, blowing so hard everyday, getting up every morning at 4 a.m., going out to work with that cold wind in your face."

"Gerald once had a sign that said 'FFA Future Farmer Lives Here,'" Freda recalled. "But when his friends went to college, he went to college too and became a CPA. Of the three, Kevin was the only one who might have been a farmer. But we were small farmers and didn't have the big machinery. I think he would have stayed if we'd had more land and more and bigger machines. He always liked those."

It was into that protective, cozy life that Kevin Saunders came squalling into the world. His extended family lived nearby—both of his grandfathers had retired from farming by the time he was old enough to know them—and his older brothers were more like indulgent uncles.

Gerald said, "Being the youngest, and having older parents, he probably wasn't disciplined as much as we were. But he got that one Saunders family trait: he is stubborn and bull-headed against all odds. It's a good trait to have."

And Kevin would later find a real need to take advantage of that family trait—that "determination to do whatever it takes."

Kevin's fragmented memories of growing up on a Kansas farm confirm the recollections of his mother and brothers. He recalls pretending to play the family player piano, stealing a friend's tiny plastic airplane and feeling bad for days, romping through the apparently endless fields of Kansas wheat, and feeling that the world had no limits in any direction.

When he started kindergarten at Downs Elementary School, he found he really liked being around the other kids, but didn't develop very good study habits because he liked fooling around too much.

Kevin's first-grade teacher, Mrs. Wiese, had a big paddle with sixteen holes in it and was a real strict lady with weathered skin and deep wrinkles. But what he remembers best about this class was "the train." It had a picture of everyone looking out the windows. The students grades determined what position they were at in the train. "If you were in the caboose, you were down to the bottom. Of course no one wanted to be in the caboose. I wasn't exactly a Rhodes Scholar back then, but I at least managed to stay out of the caboose—most of the time.

"We also had a chameleon in that class. It changed color to adapt to its environment. Funny, I still think about that chameleon, as if it had something to with my own later need in life to adapt."

It was in the first grade was that Kevin first met Jack Myers. The Myers' family farm was two and a half miles east of the Saunders farm. The two would remain life-long best friends. But after the first grade, whenever possible, teachers put Kevin and Jack in separate classes. ("We raised too much hell while we were together," Kevin admitted.)

In second grade Kevin remembers, apparently for the

first time, the sight of "big kids" throwing the football around next to the school gym.

"They could throw it so far—or so it seemed at the time. That made an impression on me. I wanted to do that, to throw that football so far until it looked like it disappeared in the Kansas sky. I liked the pads and the uniforms, I liked the idea of belonging to a team. When I saw the big guys playing football, that's what I wanted to do."

Jack Myers claims that even as early as the second or third grade that Kevin enjoyed the limelight and was telling tall tales (like the time he shot a buffalo on the farm) even back then.

Kevin's third and fourth grade classes were combined. His music teacher was Margie Loudermilk, who later married Bob Schoen and became the Saunders family historian. It was during that year that Kevin and friends Dan and Dave Renken, and Don Koops followed a time-honored tradition among Kansas farmboys and got involved in 4-H. He took part in the club's usual activities like growing vegetables or raising animals for competition, but found that these things did not satisfy his restless, animated personality.

By this time, the Saunders farm was running itself to such a degree that Donald Saunders could get more involved in his son's extra-curricular activities, including 4-H. He often accompanied Kevin on various 4-H trips. But even then, Kevin's free-spirited nature must have driven him to distraction.

"When we went on 4-H tours and shows, I just wanted to goof around," admitted Kevin.

Even so, Kevin was successful in 4-H. He was good with animals and had the grand champion bull three years out of four. One year he had both the grand champion *and* the reserve champion. Freda said that Donald was inordinately supportive of Kevin's 4-H efforts, and would stay up at the fair with him while he showed his bulls, perhaps because he wanted his son to stay and run the family farm.

Kevin believes that it was during the Mrs. Ivy

Woodward's class in the fourth grade that he first became obsessed with team sports. He remembers Jack Myers running and being faster than the rest of the boys. They played tetherball a lot at recess. "Some kids played with those big trucks and different toys like that. Not me—I couldn't stand not to feel the wind at my face. Recess always was the most important part of the day for me."

In the fifth grade, Kevin began to play Little League baseball, but it was never a passion with him like football and track, partly because Duane had excelled at the sport.

He found that he didn't like the expectations people had developed about him through their comparison of him to his brother. Kevin wanted to do his own thing— be in his own limelight, not in the shadow of his brother's—and therefore focused his energies on football and track.

Kevin finally got to play organized football as a seventh grader at Downs Junior High. Still whippet-thin and undersized, he was the team's center.

"We got our butts kicked when we were seventh graders," he said. "I remember guys pulverizing me, just great big guys. I was still just a little bitty guy when I was a seventh grader. All I remember about that team was these big monster guys hammering me into the ground, game after game.

"But for some reason, I loved it!"

Kevin went through his growth spurt between seventh and eighth grade. He began both place-kicking and punting for the football team, as well as playing tight end. He also participated in basketball and track.

The ninth grade was Kevin's first year in high school and he was a "little dog in the Big Kennel." His school had the second-ranked football team, in class 2-A, in the state his freshman year. The team had a lot of tough boys, but Kevin really enjoyed it, liked getting right in the middle and scrapping with the toughest of them. He even got to play some on varsity and the kickoff team. It was a good year for him, learning what it takes to be a champion. Even then, he realized that you've got to be tough, you've got to be able to endure whatever it takes to be a champion.

Kevin also participated in basketball and track. In track, he won the freshman mile relay, and had a fifty-eight second quarter mile as a freshman, which was impressive for his age group. He started to put on weight in his freshman year (up to 160–170 pounds) and grew close to six feet tall.

One memory in particular of Kevin's sophomores year stands out in Jack Myers' memory. While Jack was on his way to a track scholarship, Kevin just a little over average as an athlete, except in the discus. One raw April evening, the Downs track team traveled to a popular high school invitational track meet, held annually in Lincoln, Kansas.

"About ten minutes before the 440-yard dash—probably the hardest quarter of a mile in sport because you don't know if it is a sprint or a long-distance run—they ask Kevin to run it for Downs," Jack said. "Kevin doesn't have track shoes, he doesn't have spikes, all he has are soccer shoes, but he says, 'Sure, why not?'

"When it starts, I'm sitting right in the middle of the field, and Kevin takes off like it is a 100-yard dash. He's ahead of some pretty good runners. That's the way he's always been. If he runs it, he's going to go for it. At the 220-yard mark, he's still leading it, still running all out. At the 330 mark, he's *still* leading it, still running full throttle. Then, it was like a big monkey jumped on his back. He just died. But he gave it everything he had.

"Of course, Kevin didn't know how to run that race, but that wasn't going to stop him. He hadn't trained for it, he didn't have the stamina. But he said he'd do it and he gave it all he had. Which is what he's always done. And I really admired him for that. He wasn't that fast of a runner, but he always gave it all he had."

Jack has a host of similar Kevin Saunders stories, mostly illustrating Kevin's intrepid and determined spirit.

By his senior year, he was moved to quarterback on the football team. The Saunders family scrapbook is filled with articles about Kevin's senior year. He also competed in the state tournament in the discus.

Donald Saunders, however, had mixed emotions about his sons' athletic pursuits. Duane played baseball at Kansas State and Gerald ran track at Emporia State. But Kevin says that his father never did support athletics.

"He let my brothers play athletics, but he told them they ought to be working," Kevin said.

Kevin got up early each morning on the farm, drove the tractor around and around, fed the cattle, herded cattle here, herded cattle there, fed the chickens, fixed the fence, etc.—only then could he play sports.

"My dad said, 'Hell, athletics is not going to get you anywhere in life, you can work and forget about it.' But he didn't make me quit."

Perhaps as a way to mollify his father, Kevin trained in the fall by running along side his father's tractor, heaving bales of alfalfa onto a moving trailer.

One night during his senior year, according to a popular family story, Kevin staggered in at two o'clock in the morning, after drinking too much following a football victory party. Donald didn't berate his son at the time, but woke him at five o'clock for chores. On the alfalfa field, Donald slowly began increasing the speed of the tractor, forcing Kevin to work harder to keep up. After a few minutes of frenzied work, Kevin realized what was happening and grimly redoubled his efforts to keep up. Donald promptly drove even faster. Kevin—probably because he didn't have any breath to spare—refused to complain. Eventually, they completed the field in record time. Neither Kevin nor Donald mentioned the incident, but both men walked away from the now-bare field with their pride intact.

One of the early pivotal moments in Kevin's life came at his high school graduation. Bob Dole spoke at the commencement exercises for Downs High School. The school felt it was quite an honor because Mr. Dole had by that time assumed a prominent position in Washington, and Downs was a pretty small town in Kansas.

Before he arrived, the students were advised not to try and shake his right hand because of his World War II injury. Kevin was awed by Senator Dole, for all he'd accomplished, for all he'd done for Kansas, for America—and all of that with only one good arm. It made a big impact on him, that someone could do all of that with a disability.

"And since that time, I've always thought about Bob Dole, always followed his career with great interest. I heard about how much he cared for people, how much he did for people with disabilities, about how he'd always strived and worked to be the best he could be. The fact that most of that happened after he got injured proved to be a great role model for me—although I didn't know that at the time. He's still a big hero in Kansas. Everybody's real proud of him and they always say that when he retires it is going to be a sad day for Kansas."

While Kevin's best friend Jack Myers attended Oklahoma State on a football scholarship, Kevin was offered a soccer scholarship at Cloud County Community College in Concordia, Kansas.

"I thought, 'Well, I'll give it a try; see how I like it,'" Kevin said. "I'd tried soccer in high school and, to tell you the truth, I didn't like soccer because I liked more contact. After the kicks, I was always knocking guys down. My nickname was 'Mongo' because these tough guys would run into me and it was like hitting a wall. The coach didn't like it because I would just run over the other people. Sometimes the soccer ball would be there and sometimes it wouldn't. I was used to football."

After a less-than-memorable soccer career, Kevin was offered a football scholarship to Pratt Community College in Pratt, Kansas in 1975. This was more to his liking. Kevin's most memorable moment came when he made a big play and his team upset what was then the number one ranked junior college team in the nation. The score was twenty-six to twenty-five. He also participated in track and field and did well enough to get by.

The following year Kevin transferred to Kansas State where he played rugby (which was a club sport at Kansas State), joined the Alpha Tau Omega fraternity, and, on a couple of occasions, made the dean's list. He also developed what would become a lasting bond with rugby players.

Kevin majored in agricultural economics, took a number of banking courses, hoping to become an agriculture banker, and studied commodities.

"I guess the only reason I took agriculture classes was that's all I really knew. I thought it seemed like the thing to do, because I'd done it my whole life.

Upon graduation from Kansas State in 1978, Kevin began training to be a federal inspector for the United States Department of Agriculture. His ultimate goal in those days was to work with rural banks making farm loans.

He took a job with the United States Department of Agriculture as a Federal Inspector on September 9, 1978. He had a two-year training period in Corpus Christi and throughout South Texas where the field office was, but traveled extensively through South Texas and throughout the country. Whenever grain was shipped out of the country, the USDA had to be there to check that grain. Kevin volunteered to take an Instructors Training Course in Kansas City, and became a qualified instructor for the Federal Grain Inspection Service.

"My first assignment was Corpus Christi. Texas. I was a trainee Agricultural Commodity Grader. I had asked to be assigned there. A friend went down to Corpus one time during Spring Break from Kansas State and had a great time. So I went the next year at Spring Break and agreed. I thought, 'Man, that would be a great place to live.'"

Kevin's first job for the USDA was to inspect various varieties of grain in all kinds of storage facilities. Kevin was trained to evaluate both the quality and quantity of different grains.

The other significant requirement of his position was to inspect grain elevators to determine if they met government regulations regarding cleanliness and safety.

Kevin said: "There were probably forty-five employees in the USDA Federal Grain Inspection Service office in Corpus which covered everything south of San Antonio.

They sank rods and probed deep into elevators, railroad cars, trucks, and trailers to check the grain. They would take the samples using tweezers and scrape it, cut it down, and determine the quality by analyzing weight, color, and smell.

Other than the ever-present grain dust that made Kevin itch all of the time—just like when he worked in the wheat fields—Kevin enjoyed his job, including the travel up and down Texas' Gulf Coast. And, for the most part, he liked his fellow workers.

Kevin and his fellow inspectors inspected corn, wheat, soybeans, and milo in the hundreds of silos that dot South Texas. The silos on the ship channel in Corpus Christi were among the biggest in the country. The Public Grain Elevators in particular were giant-sized, holding 6.5 million bushels of grain and towering several stories above the flat coastal landscape.

Texas' far-flung empire of grain silos presented a staggering logistical problem to the federal inspection crews. Some were in dire need of maintenance, others lagged behind in safety compliance procedures, still others battled with vermin infestation. Some were owned by local businessmen who could be dealt with, others were owned by shadowy holding companies and corporations that took months to respond to even simple requests.

The Corpus Christi Port Authority Public Grain Elevators were among the biggest and, reportedly, among the safest—if the press releases from the Port Authority were to be believed. The Port Authority had only a year and a half earlier installed what it called a state-of-the-art grain dust control system.

But Kevin and the other grain inspectors weren't as sold on the safety of the silos.

"I'd made notes of the things I'd seen there," Kevin recalled. "I told the people I worked with about the problems I had found, but I didn't do the formal notification procedure each time. None of us did. In some situations, people didn't always think a formal complaint was necessary or worthwhile.

"I don't know if anybody else noticed the dust build-up—but it was a concern of mine. But I didn't push it real hard. The operators said they'd tried to get the people who built the dust collection system to come out and look at it, but that was it."

Perhaps because he didn't rock the boat at work, or perhaps it was his "gung-ho" attitude, or his brash country charm, but Kevin always seemed to get along well with his superiors and co-workers alike.

He made friends easily, from work, from the local rugby team which he joined, and from the ranks of the weightlifters that he worked out with at the health club.

Kevin also maintained contact with Jack Myers, who, after Oklahoma State, got his degree at Wichita State and eventually settled in Wichita, Kansas, where he became a superintendent for a mechanical contractor. The two continued to see each other several times a year.

Back in Corpus Christi, Kevin developed a reputation as a world-class party animal, particularly with his friends from the rugby team. He dated a number of girls in Corpus Christi and became a staple in the town's small, but lively, nightclub scene.

Then he met Brenda in his apartment complex. Despite the dismay—and occasional hostility—of his friends, Kevin impulsively married her in July of 1980.

"My rugby buddies had been against me getting married in the first place," Kevin said. "But I felt it was the right thing to do. They were all there at the wedding, of course, but none of them were in favor of my marrying. Then again, some of them may have shown up only because I asked the whole rugby team to serve as the bartenders at the reception!"

Brenda, in turn, was not happy with Kevin's rowdy friends and their evenings were often punctuated with shouts and accusations.

Among Kevin's friends was federal grain inspector Clint Black. The two spent many hours in conversation while working the night shift at the grain elevators.

"One night in March in the shack by the Corpus Christi

Public Elevator, we got caught up talking about the movie *The Other Side of the Mountain*, which is about a paralyzed skier," Kevin said. "I'd just gotten married and was horrified when the paralyzed girl's boyfriend leaves her. We kept talking, 'What would it be like to be in a wheelchair?' We talked about it for several nights."

Soon after they were married, Brenda became pregnant and the couple decided it was time to move out of the apartment. They found a modest home at 4209 Live Oak, just a few blocks off the main highway into downtown, Ocean Drive.

On clear days, you can see the Public Grain Elevator on the Corpus Christi ship channel from the front porch.

Chapter 3

Within minutes of the explosions, a general alert was issued to Neuces County physicians—the famed Code Blue. Corpus Christi Memorial Medical Center was designated as the primary trauma center and the bulk of the injured were rushed there.

An emergency call was made for neurosurgeons, orthopedic surgeons, and general surgeons to report to Memorial to assist in the evaluation and treatment of the injured. Nearly forty physicians responded.

The emergency room at Memorial Medical Center was controlled chaos. Among the bodies rushed into the hospital was Kevin Saunders. Though still alive, his vital signs indicated a coma-like state. His eyes were rolled far back in his head. A host of doctors and nurses quickly surrounded him. Snap decisions were made.

Initially, doctors were skeptical that Kevin would even live. He had a fractured skull, a collapsed lung, a broken scapula, various internal injuries, and was in critical condition—a broken back wasn't the doctor's first consideration or concern.

"I remember being conscious for brief seconds, seeing a circle of doctors around me. I could hear them talking across the table, over my body, diagnosing my injuries," said Kevin.

The physician in charge of Kevin was Dr. Charles W. Kennedy Jr., who arrived at Memorial between 4:30 or 5:00 p.m. with Dr. Frank Martin, a neurosurgeon. The two doctors drove up just after the ambulances began bringing in the injured. The men quickly pushed their way into the emergency room and began to evaluate the victim's conditions, taking advantage of the triage, and the preliminary medical evaluations and X-rays that had already been done. When both doctors turned their attention to Kevin, it was soon obvious that Kevin's condition was both an orthopedic and neurological type of problem.

Because of the severity of Kevin's injuries and the indication from the X-rays that the injury to the spinal cord was devastating—so much so that any early surgery would be of little assistance —the doctors' major concern was to stabilize Kevin and make sure there were no additional or potential complications. And then later, to perform surgery on an elective basis, to examine more closely the damage to Kevin's spine.

Poking and prodding amid the torn and burned flesh, Dr. Kennedy first found a vein for an IV line and then inserted a catheter. Kennedy and Martin accompanied Kevin upstairs to the Intensive Care Unit at the hospital, where he was placed in a "roto-bed" to further protect the internal and skeletal injuries.

The roto-bed is like a moveable, form-fitting casket with pads keeping the arms and legs spread. His condition at first was too unstable to be placed in the more permanent "Stryker frame."

"The roto-bed slowly tilted left and right, moving all the time, a little at a time, like a clock," Kevin said. "And all the while I was attached to every tube and hose imaginable."

The first X-ray seemed to indicate that there would be paralysis. In some back-injury cases the fracture has minimal displacement and the doctors have to decide whether or not they want to do something to get pressure off the broken spinal cord. In Kevin's case, his spine was both broken and offset approximately T-5 (thoracic 5), which meant a loss of feeling from the sternum down.

The doctors therefore understood that there was little hope of repairing the damage to the spinal cord, and that the most they could do was stabilize the fracture to prevent further injury.

After waiting two weeks for Kevin to stabilize in ICU, the two men operated on Kevin for nearly five hours. Dr.

Martin handled most of the decompression and Dr. Kennedy removed bone fragments.

"In intensive care, while in something like a coma, I thought I heard the doctors saying that they were going to let me die," Kevin said. "I heard they didn't think I was gonna live. It scared me. I didn't want to die, I wanted to live. I kept fighting, I was so scared. Maybe that's why I didn't die. But it was close."

As soon as news spread about the explosion at the Corpus Christi Public Elevator, Brenda, frantic, tried to find Kevin. At last a hospital administrator at Memorial confirmed that Kevin had been admitted. Kevin's mother-in-law, who had joined her daughter shortly after the first news reports on the explosion, called Donald and Freda Saunders and told them the bad news. The Saunders had originally heard about the explosion on the national news, but didn't know that Kevin was involved until she called.

Duane Saunders, who was on active duty with the reserves in San Antonio, was the first member of the Saunders family to arrive at Kevin's bedside.

Ironically, Duane had heard something about a grain elevator explosion in Corpus Christi on the news and vaguely wondered if Kevin might have been involved. But it wasn't until a couple hours later that his commanding officer found him and said, "Your brother's been injured." All Col. Lucas said was, "You need to get down there." He didn't say how bad Kevin was.

Duane arrived in Corpus that evening and went straight to the hospital. Duane found Kevin, drifting in and out of consciousness, in his rotating "roto-bed" and listed in critical condition.

Although Dr. Kennedy couched his words as carefully as possible, there was by now no doubt in his mind that Kevin faced possible paralysis. He first took Duane, then Brenda, aside and detailed Kevin's prospects for walking again.

He told them that he and Dr. Martin did not have any hopes that there was going to be improvement, but that they were going to try and stabilize the spine so that at least he would have good sitting balance and that he would possibly be able to do some transfers and ambulations—but that they felt that their initial job was to do the surgical stabilizations and make sure that no other complications were developing.

Despite what the doctors said, Duane hoped against hope that Kevin's spinal cord was somehow intact. The swelling was so severe in first X-rays that it was not one hundred percent certain that the vertebrae had indeed separated completely. Unfortunately, later X-rays left little doubt.

When Duane met his parents at the airport the following day, he tried to break the news to them gently. Donald and Freda Saunders were at first relieved—their initial report was that Kevin was near death—but the possibility that he might be paralyzed profoundly affected the two.

"When I saw him, I didn't know what to think," Freda said. "I got sick—from the worry, I guess."

Duane Saunders was forced to return to San Antonio the following day after making sure his parents were settled in Corpus Christi. Over the next few days, the Saunders would go to the hospital, then return to Kevin's apartment to watch the coverage of the aftermath of the elevator explosion. Each day that Kevin survived the night took him one step further away from the grave.

After it was certain that Kevin would survive, Kevin's parents called Jack Myers' parents in Downs. They in turn called Jack in Wichita who got a plane ticket and flew out that afternoon to Corpus Christi.

"I walked into his hospital room where they had him upside down strapped to the bed. I could hear him BS-ing with the nurse, asking her something like if she'd ever seen a tornado or something. This was several days after the accident. I turned around, went out, and cried for about fifteen minutes.

"I had heard that he was paralyzed, but I hadn't known how bad he looked. It just got to me. Luckily, he didn't see me, I turned around and walked out before he had a chance to.

"His shoulder was broken, they had a back strap under his chin, and they had him strapped in. There was lots of swelling in his face, especially around his ears and neck. I was expecting because of the explosion that he'd be burned. So in that regard, he did not look as bad as I had anticipated."

"After the initial surgery, the doctors waited to make sure the wounds were OK, then took him back to surgery where they placed a body jacket on him.

After Kevin came out of his near coma-like state, he was understandably disoriented. He was heavily drugged. It all seemed like a dream to him—or more like a nightmare. He was lying there, heavily sedated, and asking himself what happened. He was in and out of consciousness.

"If you've ever had a dream that scared you so much you couldn't move, or a nightmare that was so frightening that you tried to will yourself to wake up—well, that's exactly what I thought was happening to me. I thought it was just one of those kind of dreams."

Kevin's stamina enabled him to make slow, steady progress. First Dr. Kennedy ordered the gradual lessening of the pain-killing medicine—although it would be months before he would be off it completely. Then he had Kevin moved out of intensive care. Without the pain-killers, Kevin slowly regained control.

When Kevin was strong enough, after about two weeks, Kennedy took him to surgery to insert an instrument called a Harrington rod, which had originally been designed for use in the treatment of scoliosis. The Harrington rod was placed on the outside of the spine and was held in place with a system of hooks. Kennedy also fused the bones in Kevin's back with a bone removed from his hip.

It was after that surgery that Kevin finally accepted what he'd suspected for the past two weeks: He'd never walk again.

At first he still didn't want to accept the reality, he wanted to deny that anything had happened. By that time, Kevin was in one of the Stryker frames—a rotating bed that had him sandwiched face down. People would come in to visit him, squat down underneath, and look up at him.

"That's when I first remember thinking, 'Man, what the hell has happened to me?' That's when I knew I was in some serious trouble."

Kevin's doctors decided to break him in gently. They told him first that the elevator was fifty to seventy-five percent destroyed and that several people had died. But he was only interested in hearing why he was in the Stryker frame—and why he couldn't feel his legs.

Finally, Dr. Kennedy came in and said, "Kevin, I hate to tell you this, but your spinal cord was severed and the chances are that you won't be able to walk again. You'll be confined to a wheelchair for the rest of your life."

"I screamed, 'No way! That can't be right!' I was mad. Who wouldn't be mad in a situation like that? I was angry at the doctor because who was he to tell me that? Who's he to say I won't walk again? He's not God."

For several days, Kevin was torn between towering rages, impotent depression, and troubled, uneasy sleep. He refused to accept Dr. Kennedy's assessment that he would probably be paralyzed for life.

He was immobilized in the Stryker frame for about three weeks. It seemed to him that time just dragged on forever. He didn't know day and night. "Imagine being sandwiched like that and you need something to drink— you're there at the mercy of other people. It's a horrifying feeling."

Donald and Freda stayed in Corpus Christi several weeks. Kevin would talk to them sometimes, but rarely remembered what he had said.

Kevin continued to grow frustrated, both at his condition and his inability to communicate. The head injuries, the narcotics, the despair, and the pain caused him to struggle with even simple words.

He remembers people coming up to him and how he would ask them for water. However, in intensive care he was not supposed to have any water. "I was dying of thirst and no one would give me water. Finally, I told them if they couldn't give me any water then don't bother me, leave me alone. That's one of the big things I remember about being in intensive care. I never did find out why I couldn't have any."

Each night, lying suspended in air, often face down toward the black floor, Kevin brooded over his fate. He remembered playing rugby or football, running with the Kansas wind in his face. He remembered romping with his pack of mutts. But mostly he remembered walking.

"I just didn't believe what they said, that I was paralyzed," Kevin said. "I just couldn't believe my legs wouldn't work again, that I'd never walk again. It was denial. I just *knew* that my legs were gonna work again and I didn't care what they said.

Night after night Kevin would try to sleep, but all he could think about was all that he had lost. He'd get depressed and angry about the whole situation and everything that had happened. He would replay the explosion over and over in his mind. Then he would forget where he was for a moment in the dark, start to roll over to get up, but couldn't move in the Stryker frame. And it would all come back to him again.

He would lose track of time—wouldn't remember in the dark if he were turned upside down or right side up. He couldn't tell how many hours would elapse before a nurse would come in and turn him over to keep him from getting bed sores. "It wasn't much fun, I guarantee that. All the positions were boring. You'd finally fall asleep, then a nurse would come in during the night and flip you like a pancake, waking you up, and the whole thing would start again."

Gradually, as the weeks wore on, Kevin said that he quit thinking about the big things that he'd lost and began to dwell on what he'd never be able to do.

He had just gotten married seven months before the

explosion and had just signed the escrow papers on the house—it was the first house he had ever bought.

"My wife and I had just found out that she was two-weeks pregnant, and on the day of the explosion, I was thinking about leaving work early and buying a swing set or a baby crib, and I wanted to go by the new house to see if they'd fit. The explosion was at 3:10 p.m., and I wanted to go by the house one more time.

"I should have gone.

"Then I'd think about my baby again, how I'd planned to play with him—or her. I kept thinking about the things I'd never get to do now: play catch, jump up and touch the rim of the basketball goal, teach him how to ride a bike, show him how to kick a football or get down in a three-point stance... I got more depressed the more I thought about all of the things I couldn't do. I went through all of that over and over again in my mind. Over and over again."

Despite his emotional anguish, Kevin's physical condition slowly continued to improve. Once Dr. Kennedy was certain there were no lingering physical problems—all of the bones were knitting nicely—he had Kevin moved to a private room.

Once there, Kennedy had Kevin measured for a body cast. Technicians made the plaster mold of his body, from the neck to the legs, and made the cast from those fittings. His stay in the Stryker frame had been, in part, to immobilize him in preparation for the body cast.

Kevin nicknamed his cast "the turtle shell." And though his freedom of movement was little better than it was in the Stryker frame, at least he could be pushed around the hospital in a wheelchair and visit with the other patients.

Five weeks had elapsed since the explosion.

"When I was a little stronger, I went down to see a friend from the accident who ended up dying seven weeks later, Albert Tripp. He was about fifty, had a nice family, several kids. He had a look about him like he was already gone. He was stronger than me, but he had a severe head injury. He couldn't talk, he just had a funny look on his face."

Although it didn't seem like it to Kevin, life was indeed going on outside of Memorial Hospital. While he was struggling to accept his new role, the recriminations and accusations were heating up in the aftermath of the grain elevator explosion.

When it was clear that Kevin would live, he found himself surrounded by a whole roomful of lawyers and/ or their attractive secretaries. "All of those lawyers instinctively knew that this was a big money deal. So to get me to sign with them, the lawyers would send their secretaries. They'd talk to me a long time. And if any of them knew friends of mine, they tried to use that friendship to get to me."

But Kevin said that one person who came to the hospital less and less to visit was his wife, Brenda. He told himself that it was because she was pregnant or that it was too painful for her to see him so badly hurt. "It still didn't do a whole lot for my self-esteem. Our marriage just seemed to fall apart after the accident. I guess it never was very strong enough to begin with, and this was just what it took to push it over the edge."

Eventually, Dr. Kennedy and Kevin's other consulting doctors agreed that he was strong enough to be moved to a rehabilitation hospital. They took Kevin by ambulance to Houston as soon as he was stabile enough. When he arrived at the Texas Institute of Rehabilitation and Research, he couldn't even sit up by himself, he had been bed-ridden for so long. And when he finally did sit up, he couldn't remain upright for very long at all.

At this point, Kevin had little desire to begin physical therapy. The slightest movement was a strenuous effort for him and left him yearning to return to bed to rest.

In addition to being trapped in a body cast, weak as a kitten, and paralyzed from the shoulders down, the shattered scapula meant that Kevin couldn't use his left arm at all and had virtually no strength in his right arm.

At the Institute, Kevin saw people whose injuries were more debilitating than his own. He also saw people who were doing well, people who were overcoming those disabilities who would say to him, "You can do that too!" And so began Kevin's long, arduous, frustrating—but rewarding—journey into the world of occupational and physical therapy.

"It's a tough place to go. The nurses and the people there are tough. I know they have probably been told to make the patients do everything they possibly can on their own. But that doesn't make the tasks any easier. They leave you in your wheelchair at your bedside and tell you, 'Get in the bed!' When you can hardly use your arms and you're in a body cast paralyzed from the chest down—you don't know how to do that. Somebody may as well tell you to jump across the Grand Canyon. You just feel helpless."

Kevin saw many things at the hospital that were both motivating and frustrating. He saw an elderly lady pushing eight pounds over her head when he couldn't even lift his arm over his head. He saw a thirty-eight-year-old lady pumping forty pounds over her head like it was nothing, all the while sitting in a wheelchair.

So he went to the weight room and discovered that he couldn't even lift his arm off his chest. "Or I'd lift a pound, then I'd I go, 'Jesus, I just wanna pass out. I just give up. This is too hard. This hurts too much.' You're so far down you don't see any way of digging your way out of the hole. And each day the physical therapists would say, 'You used to be an athlete, can't you even do this?'"

Kevin's first physical challenge was to get out of bed, into his wheelchair, and push himself around the hospital.

That was great progress for him, just being able to get up and go somewhere. After a few weeks, he could feed himself and drink his own juice. Those little successes encouraged him enough to move onto more significant recoveries, like the use of his arms. He lifted different weights, lying down on the mats and pushing up or rolling side to side, all with his body cast on. Kevin said he felt like some giant turtle.

He was still having trouble with his shoulder. The doctors wanted to operate but his brother Duane advised against it. Over time, Kevin regained the use of his arms with only a slight loss in his range of motion.

Duane was able to visit Kevin more often than any other family member. His burgeoning physical therapy consulting company often took him from his Minneapolis home to seminars and speaking engagements in Texas. Whenever he was near, Duane would go directly to the TIRR. There he would encourage Kevin to face all the challenges before him: his rehab, his career, his education.

"He really pushed me with my therapy. Finally, I said, 'Hey, you don't know until you're in here.' I would get so mad because I'd try, but I just couldn't do it. But he never stopped pushing.

"Physical therapists are like that: push, push, push. They never cut you any slack. I think some people need to decide in their own time when they want to do things. When you're hurting that badly, and your body has been so mangled and so changed, it's just hard to want to do all of those things—even for a guy like me who had been an athlete. I wanted to do it. But sometimes I just wanted to lay there. I just didn't care.

"I realize now that pushing was what I needed, but at the time, I was going to do it when I felt like doing it! But hospitals can't afford to give you the luxury of doing things on your own."

The longer Kevin was at the TIRR, the more his resentment built. He now attributes it to the onset of depression and frustration over his fate, but at the time he needed someone to lash out at.

Kevin, who before the accident had been an active and independent person, found it extremely hard to be trapped in a controlled environment where the staff were constantly telling him to "do this, eat that," etc. Sometimes he would refuse to cooperate, just to maintain some sense of self-determination and identity.

"I'd get mad, I would just want to kill someone. They wanted me to do more than I could do. I'd sit on the side of my bed for—I don't know, maybe hours—because by then I didn't even know how to *want* to try!

"Other guys felt the same. They put this odometer on your wheelchair so they could tell how many miles you put in during rehab. Some guys would put their chairs on a block and turn their wheels with their hands while they lay in bed watching TV. That's what the nurses and counselors were up against."

Kevin, at least, didn't violently oppose his therapists and nurses. He remembers Haden Harris, a giant high school football player who refused to believe he'd been paralyzed and would fight with the staff, and scream at the doctors, "I don't care what you say! Damn it! I'm *going to walk*! Ain't nothing going to keep me down here, I'm getting out of this damn bed."

"As for me, I tried and tried and tried to get my toes to move. Sometimes I'd shout, 'I think I got something moving!' I just wanted so bad to believe that I would walk again. You can't imagine what a feeling that is. And everybody in there was going through exactly the same thing. Each one of them had a doctor come to them and say, 'I'm sorry, but you're never going to walk again.' It's just hard to believe that when there is nothing wrong with your legs, that your spinal cord can't get any messages to them to tell them to walk."

Kevin was in the TIRR for seven months. For much of that time he lay motionless in his bed, glaring at the ever-present PTs and nurses, avoiding rehab whenever possible.

His bills were paid by the insurance company. And there was a steady trickle of visitors, despite his brooding personality. Finally, the doctors began offering the hope of weekend passes for a certain amount of rehab work accomplished. Kevin grudgingly began to put in the necessary hours.

One person who was conspicuous by her absence was Brenda. Kevin attributed it to the fact that she was in the late stages of pregnancy. The prospect of seeing his new baby gave Kevin added incentive to be able to leave the TIRR to go to Corpus Christi for the birth.

Steven Duane Saunders was born on December 16,

1981 at Spohn Hospital in Corpus Christi, where Kevin had been temporarily transferred to be present for the birth.

Steven's birth proved to be an impetus. Kevin's physical therapists found a more willing patient in the days that followed. His focus had begun to shift from what he couldn't do to what he could. Finally, he began to throw himself into his physical therapy.

Some of his old rugby buddies helped a lot, especially Robert Hays. Also, Jack Myers flew down from Kansas to be with Kevin whenever he could. Kevin could see the pain they felt whenever they were with him written on their faces.

"They would see me and remember that, just days ago, we were pounding bodies. Then all of a sudden, there I was, in the hospital, barely able to get out of bed. The whole team made a special effort to be there for me. They were my brothers, no doubt about it."

And finally, during his sometimes aimless spins through the TIRR wards, Kevin encountered Mique Davis. Mique was paralyzed from the neck down after a diving accident. But Mique was different than any quadriplegic Kevin had ever met.

"Mique was always drawing beautiful pictures," Kevin said. "You'd ask him how it was going and he'd say, 'Hey, it's going great. Feeling good today. *Beautiful* day today.' That was his attitude—and the guy was paralyzed from the neck down! He was drawing with his pen and pencil between his teeth. I just couldn't believe it. That was a guy with a positive attitude about life. I remembered that."

Eventually, Kevin regained some of his old vitality. He became a popular figure in the many halls of the TIRR, laughing, joking, encouraging other patients. His mastery of the wheelchair became such that he was used as a model by the doctors and physical therapists.

One afternoon, Kevin wheeled two blocks to a convenience store at the TIRR annex (still in his body cast) to get a tube of toothpaste. Three men blocked his way and said, "Hey, man, you got any money?" When

Kevin tried to pass, they demanded all his money. "Hey, I've only got three dollars," Kevin said. The men shrugged and grabbed it from him. That was the last time Kevin went out for toothpaste alone.

Still, his trips to Corpus Christi became more and more frequent until, about seven months after he was first admitted, Kevin was released from the Texas Institute for Rehabilitation and Research.

The date was March 16, 1982.

Unfortunately, it was a bittersweet parting. For one thing, he would be forever hooked to a catheter and would have reoccurring bladder and bowel problems. But perhaps more disturbing, as his counselors had tried to warn him, life outside the TIRR was more difficult than he had dreamed.

"The world from a wheelchair is tough!" Kevin said. "It was kind of amazing to me. Chairbound, you're on your own in the walking world. If you can make it, fine. If you can't, there's no one who'll worry about it. In '82, most public places had no accessibility for the handicapped. "

Kevin was irritated by the way people would stare at him, and pry—ask him questions like "what's your problem?" or worse still, talk over him as if he wasn't there.

"One time, right after I got out of the hospital, I was in a store and I politely told a man 'Excuse me' because I couldn't get by. The guy whirled around, glared at me, and snarled, 'Screw you, crip. Go around!'"

There were other problems, particularly at home. The tension with Brenda was almost unbearable. The two spent most nights in silence broken only by angry accusations. Simple discussions quickly disintegrated into bitter quarrels.

Earlier, when Kevin had come back to Corpus on weekend passes from the TIRR still in his body cast, his wife would promptly leave him with baby Steven. She'd disappear for hours, leaving him to care for a baby he could hardly bend over to reach.

Occasionally, the Corpus Christi television stations would come by to chronicle Kevin's recovery. On those days, the Saunders would put on their best clothes and best smiles and face the cameras like the ideal couple.

In one such segment, Kevin told how they were planning to move to a bigger house, with wheelchair-accessible doors and ramps. He told how he was going to buy Brenda a two-carat ring, and he praised her for standing by him when many other patients at the Texas Institute for Rehabilitation had had their wives leave them.

In another such feature, Kevin is shown preparing for one of the three baths he was forced to take each day in an effort to increase circulation. He told the reporter that he was planning to go to law school, while his wife was planning on attending nursing school.

In each segment, Steven—who is a mirror image of his mother—crawls happily around the foreground, the product of what is apparently a happy marriage.

"But that's not the way it was at all," Kevin said. "Appearances can be deceiving. My life at home was hell. One night Brenda broke a lot of plates and glasses in the kitchen by throwing them at me. Another time she broke the telephone over my head, knocking me out of my wheelchair. Still another time, she came up on me from behind while I was in my body cast, hit me, and catapulted me out of my chair. I was going to take a bath and didn't have any clothes on and I had to crawl from the hallway back into the bathroom. But I guess I wasn't too pleasant to live with, either. This was coming at the end of a rocky road."

Eventually, Kevin did return to school in the Fall of 1983. He took graduate classes at Corpus Christi State University with the idea of working toward an MBA in business administration.

"At first I did it just to see if I could make it in the world," he said. "I wanted to see if I could go back to school and make the grade. After a couple of years, I didn't finish. I lacked only nine hours, but I showed myself and everyone else that I could do it. The only reason I quit was that I got bored with school. No other reason."

One of the reasons that Kevin grew bored with school was that life in the real world was growing more interesting by the day. It appeared that the legal action involving the grain elevator explosion was going to be on an unprecedented scale—and Kevin was going to be a star participant.

Chapter 4

When the lawyers—and their attractive secretaries—continued to call almost daily on the Saunders' household, Kevin realized it was time to make a decision.

He finally called a buddy of his from college, Kimball Simpson, an attorney in Dallas. He told him what was happening, so Kimball checked around and then recommended a lawyer named Joe Jamail—said he was the best. Joe was very interested and flew a representative to Kevin in a matter of hours.

Joe Jamail, even then, was considered one of the best-known personal injury lawyers in the country. He would later achieve national attention for being on the winning side of the landmark Pennzoil vs. Texaco suit. But that level of notoriety meant that Joe had a number of cases running concurrently. So Jamail in turn called an old friend in Corpus Christi, Guy Allison, to serve as point man for the case.

Guy was already handling several cases related to the explosion, including personal-injury clients and the grain elevator itself (which had suffered an estimated $28 million worth of damage). It was very relatively simple to coordinate Kevin's case along with all of the rest of them.

The entry of Jamail into the fray caused proceedings to quicken to a rapid pace. Kevin agreed with the standard 60/40 split on any award.

"My case was the first to be settled out of court because I had the big-time lawyer—*Mr.* Joe Jamail—so he's the guy that got them to shake first," Kevin said. "After they settled with me, then everyone started getting theirs. He's the guy that got the tree to shake."

Even before the various lawyers began to huddle on Kevin, events were coming to a head that assigned plenty of blame—and gave Guy plenty of cause for optimism.

The day after the blast, Port of Corpus Christi director Harry Plomarity told the *Corpus Christi Caller-Times* that he would "welcome" an inspection by the Occupational Health and Safety Administration.

That same day, Port Commissioner Thomas Sexton told the *Caller-Times* that he was "disappointed" with the performance of the $4 million dust control system, which had been installed the previous year.

"The commissioners felt we had the safest grain house on the Gulf Coast," Sexton is reported as saying. "We didn't cut any corners in the dust control system."

Fires were still smoldering the following day and only four of what would ultimately be nine bodies had been found. Two smaller fires blazed up hours after the initial explosion, but were quickly contained.

An investigator for the National Academy of Sciences, Charles W. Kaufman, eventually released a statement claiming that the explosion was caused by accumulated grain dust in the conveyor belt system.

Kaufman said the grain dust allegedly gathered under the metal hoods covering the belts.

"We saw the grain dust when the conveyor belt was torn apart," Kaufman told *The Corpus Christi Caller-Times*. "In the area between the spout's end and the metal hood cover was about four to six inches of grain dust. It accounted for a lot of dust... hidden dust. Grain dust they [port officials] didn't know was there.

"You could see how the explosion traveled down the conveyors, splitting the metal covers and spewing dust in the basement," he said.

But a later study funded by the Port of Corpus Christi said the exact cause of the 1981 explosion would never be known.

William Clarke, a consulting engineer from Toledo, Ohio, told the *Caller-Times:*

"In spite of extensive searches at the site and review of the material obtained, we are unable to determine the exact cause of initial ignition or location of initial explosion."

Another study commissioned by the report came from Robert Anderson, another Toledo-based grain elevator engineer. Anderson's report blamed a worn bearing at the base of an elevator leg for the explosion and subsequent fire.

But Clarke's report places the original explosion in or near bin 149 in the C-house—about six hundred feet away from Anderson's point of origin.

Anderson instead theorized that vents and passageways channeled the fire to the C-house location postulated by Clarke.

Clarke's report claimed that the accumulation of grain dust was a contributing factor to the expanding of the explosion. After a bin had been filled or partially filled, it could not be entered for four to eight hours because the thickness of the grain dust prevented breathing or seeing.

"Unless you accept the bearing theory given by Mr. Anderson, I think that this explosion, as have so many others, will go down as cause unknown," said Col. Nolan Rhodes, the director of engineering for the port.

In 1981, the National Academy of Sciences issued a statement saying that, of the 250 elevator and mill explosions in 1980, 103 were reported to have been started by "unknown causes."

"But to my way of thinking, we never did really did try the case that was, in my mind, the cause, which was the Phostoxin—the pesticide," Guy said. "I really think that was probably the ignition source, but it was an enormous detective story to try to figure out what the ignition source was. Of course, all you had to have had is one guy lighting a cigarette that didn't know any better and the whole case is gone."

After the lines had been drawn and the experts called in, Kevin spent months answering questions for lawyers representing the various parties:

The lawyers asked questions like: Where were you? What do you remember? Was the ground shaking? Where was this? Where was that? Could you draw a diagram of this? With the one hand he could use, they had him draw a diagram of where he was at the time of the explosion, the elevator, where he thought the explosions started, and other questions concerning his knowledge of the elevator.

Kevin earned a good reputation as a witness and a client for his willingness to help, whether it was for him or whether it was for some other dead or injured person in the case. He was very available, which was not all that uncommon, but it was a sign of the new positive attitude that Kevin was developing.

Jamail and Allison created a complex, sophisticated game plan to maximize Kevin's earning potential. Some defendants were dealt with privately, others publicly. Some were urged to settle out of court, others were challenged to face a public trial.

"The people that gave up the control of their cases to the insurance carrier did not do as well," said Guy. "Kevin's case, the De Los Santos case, the grain elevator case, and two of the dead cases, that we had direct control over, prospered much better than the rest of them. The rest of them fared well."

As a result of the lawyers' plan, media coverage of the settlement phase of the various complaints is spotty. Some of the major settlements were never reported, by agreement between the two parties.

But one settlement that was made public caught the attention of the other defendants in a big way. Orchestrated by Joe Jamail, the coverage was designed to put pressure on the remaining defendants to settle— quickly and quietly.

A *Corpus Christi Caller Times* account of the hearing [headlined "Crowd of lawyers is here for hearing on grain-blast suits"] by Jerry Winkler in 1982 likened the mass of lawyers at the courthouse to "a heavy day of trading on the floor of the New York Stock Exchange.

"Men in business suits shuffled around the main jury room of the Nueces County courthouse. Whispering in small groups, the more than thirty lawyers of plaintiffs and defendants quietly discussed details of multimillion-dollar agreements while various attorneys spelled out how more than $8 million would be paid to four victims or their survivors."

Judge Joe Wade of Beeville approved the settlements, then permitted the four cases to be separated from a consolidated suit brought by nine other plaintiffs and their families. The plaintiffs were suing various firms involved in the design, construction, and installation of equipment at the Public Elevator.

Judge Wade told the massed group of lawyers that the October 4, 1982 trial date stood for the suit by the nine plaintiffs who had not settled. Wade also rejected a request for a change of venue entered by several of the defendants' lawyers.

Carter-Day was the only company reaching a settlement in the four victims' cases.

"The settlement, in essence, separates legal action on behalf of four plaintiffs—Albert Tripp and Robert Valdez, both of whom died in the blast; Manuel De Los Santos; and Saunders—from the nine other cases," Winkler wrote. "Under the agreement with the four plaintiffs, Carter-Day and the Port of Corpus Christi would join in legal action against other defendants."

The agreement offered Carter-Day an opportunity to share in any eventual damages awarded against the remaining companies being sued.

The agreement was to also name Dreyfus Grain Co. as a defendant in the case within thirty days. That addition involved allegations that Dreyfus had delivered smoldering grain to the elevator prior to the fatal fire and explosion.

In releasing the port from further litigation by the four, the agreement required the port to pay $80,000 to the survivors of Tripp. The port was still a defendant in a suit by victims who were not port-elevator employees.

According to Van Huseman, the attorney representing CEA Carter-Day, the four cases in the settlement involved "the worst of the cases and, in our opinion, the highest-powered lawyers."

Winkler reported that the settlement awarded between $3.5 and $4 million to Kevin, his family, and his attorney.

Carter-Day also agreed to reimburse insurance companies which had already paid Kevin compensation and medical expenses.

As television cameras whirred around him, Joe Jamail grandly announced that, as a part of the settlement, Kevin would receive an annuity of $84,000 for himself and his wife for twenty years or life, whichever was greater.

Joe said that Kevin could receive benefits totaling more than eighteen million dollars, with $1,850,000 due within forty-five days. Carter-Day's part of the medical bills had already totaled to between $300,000 and $500,000.

Although no one knew it at the time, the annuity proved to be the most important part of the entire settlement, not the more flashy figure of $18 million. Kevin gives Guy Allison full credit for insisting on the annuity—or "structures."

"I have always encouraged—and I probably have a thousand clients that have annuities—clients who are not sophisticated investors to do something like that, either set up an annuity or an irrevocable, spendthrift type of trust." Guy had not assumed that Kevin would waste the money, that wasn't his fear. In his experience, the way his clients lose their money is through some friend that has an investment that they think is going to be a big deal—but goes sour. Or they loan it to friends or to relatives. But when the money is put in a trust or annuity, it is out of the individual's hands, and they don't have to worry about investing it. Plus, when that friend or relative asks for money, they can say, "I put all of that in a trust, I don't have any control over it." It's easier to say no.

Of Kevin's settlement, forty percent went to Jamail, along with all expenses, right off the top. It was all tax-free. An annuity was set up that started off at $6,669, the payments compounded annually to take care of Steven's future college education at $1,500 per month for four years when he turned eighteen. When he turned twenty-one, he would get $50,000 and at age twenty-five, another $100,000. Kevin also put $250,000 in a trust account fund for Steven's future.

Later, the same original four plaintiffs—the families of Tripp and Valdez, along with Saunders and De Los Santos—settled with the company that had supplied elevator equipment for the Public Elevator.

Although exact terms of the settlement were not released to the public, Visiting Judge Stanley Kirk of Houston, found against Combustion Engineering, Inc. and the Ersham Co. According to the suit, Combustion Engineering Inc., and the Ersham Co. provided the Port of Corpus Christi with defective machinery—particularly a bearing house on a conveyor belt—that was suspected of causing the blast.

The various trials and out-of-court settlements continued until 1985. Albert Tripp's survivors received a $1.08 million award with additional funds to be repaid by Carter-Day for medical expenses already covered by the health insurer and the workman's compensation agency, according to the *Corpus Christi-Caller-Times*.

Survivors of Joe Valdez, an assistant superintendent of the public elevator, received between $850,000 and $900,000.

Carter-Day, which made and installed the dust control system at the elevator, is paying the largest portion of the settlements.

The port also is named as a defendant in the suit, but has a liability limit not to exceed $300,000. *Caller-Times* reporters Jerry Winkler and Bruce Millar reported that, as part of the Carter-Day agreement, the port's insurance carrier recovered $18.7 million for property damage to the elevator.

"The port has settled its claims from the disaster," port attorney M. Harvey Weil told the *Caller-Times*, a figure that included property damage, grain loss, and compensation for interruption of business.

"The port's insurance settlement totaled $27.9 million, of which $18.7 million was to be recovered in the Carter-Day agreement. The port has earmarked its settlement funds for rebuilding the elevator, and it is expected to cover construction costs with the facility to be in operation by July 1983."

Also receiving $3 million from Carter-Day was Manuel De Los Santos, a port employee who suffered severe head, chest and abdominal injuries and burns in the blast.

"We didn't settle the last of those cases until about 1985," Guy said. "I don't really think 'dragging on' is an accurate overview. What was happening was that we put together an extremely sophisticated plan to sequentially settle cases that evolved beyond our wildest dreams as far as the benefits to the client.

"We didn't want to settle them all at the same time because there is more money blaming other defendants sequentially. In other words, if you focus on a particular defendant, they know they're going to get stuck and when you settle with them, then you go focus on somebody else. It was sort of a battle plan. As it turned out, it worked out beyond our wildest hopes.

"Kevin was a person that was easy to want to help because he was a person that was obviously extremely motivated and while he was crushed with the loss, the physical loss, unlike some people, Kevin was ready to look ahead rather than look back. I don't think there is any better example floating around my office for the value of a system where someone, who is injured through the negligence of someone else, can be compensated for their loss. Kevin got some awfully good recovery money and used it to rehab himself."

Of course, in the end, it was *only* money—even though there was a lot of it. But Kevin's interviews at the time of the first settlement were positive.

"You've got to be as happy as you can. That money kind of makes it easier to live with.

"I used to be able to go to the show and go to the racquetball club. Now I can buy the racquetball club."

But, as he told a television station, "$4 million can't give you your legs back."

A document from October 21, 1982 is revealing. On Jamail, Kolius & Mithoff letterhead, it details the agreement between Saunders and CEA Carter-Day Co.:

Total Annuity Settlement $1,250,000.00
Total Settlement $1,830,000.00
Total $3,080,000.00
Attorney's Fee $1,230,000.00
Gross to Client $600,000.00
Expenses
100% case expenses ($362.78)
David Perry Expenses ($7,590.00)
Total Expenses $7,953.22
Net to Client $592,046.78
Advances to Texas Commerce Bank $11,635.68
Final Check to Client $580,411.10

The statement was approved and signed by Joseph D. Jamail.

In this, as in every instance, Kevin's part of the take would be much smaller than the public's perception of what he actually received.

Chapter 5

"The settlement gave me a sense of power," Kevin said. "I'd lost my sense of manhood when I became injured. I was completely paralyzed from the chest down. I couldn't feel anything; I couldn't move anything. Each day I was more devastated.

"Trouble was, I'd just made $18 million and I went home to somebody who wasn't glad to see me.

The difficulties between Kevin and Brenda increased while he was recuperating at home. She would sometimes vent her frustrations physically. The settlement didn't change things very much. Kevin tried buying her things: a ring that cost $15,000, and a fur coat that cost $7,000. He gave money to her family. But none of it seemed to Kevin to change things between them for the better.

Still, at his wife's insistence, the couple made plans to move to a bigger, more elaborate house in Corpus Christi's exclusive Buckingham Estates. Once they found the right house—to the tune of $450,000—Kevin left the planning of the house to his wife, who threw herself into decorating the interior. Eventually, however, the excitement of designing a new house paled.

"I never met her until after the accident," Jack Myers said. "They'd only been married a few months when the accident occurred. You can probably see both sides of the story. Still, my wife and I went down to visit after the accident, but we left early because Brenda was raising so much hell."

On another occasion, while Kevin's parents were visiting, an enraged daughter-in-law slammed a chair repeatedly into a wall before storming out of the house.

Freda Saunders was taken aback.

One day after Kevin had been home from TIRR for about nine months, he and Brenda were driving with Steven, still just a little baby, between them in the car. Looking straight ahead she said, "I'm leaving and going to live with my sister in Beaumont."

"I'd heard she'd been dating some guy there, and she said when I was in the hospital in Houston a young doctor gave her a ride in his Porsche and stuff. I didn't need to hear that, but she told me anyway. She said she was leaving to go live with her sister and she wanted everything she was entitled to by law."

Kevin knew enough about lawyers and settlements by now to know that a divorce would ruin him—that the only people who would really get what they were "entitled" to by law, were the lawyers themselves. Something inside Kevin finally snapped.

"I turned to her and shouted, 'You bitch!' She turned and hit me in the face again and again. She'd been doing this for a year, even when I couldn't do anything to defend myself. But this time I was strong enough to hit her back. So I did. I was sorry, but I just blew up.

"She left that day."

Kevin asked a friend to recommend to him a good divorce attorney, who suggested a man named Scott Cook. Scott's reaction to Kevin's story was immediate: "I suggest you file suit immediately. If you don't, she's going to establish residency in Houston or out of town and you will end up going there to fight a lawsuit for divorce."

Reluctantly, Kevin filed a petition for divorce in Corpus Christi.

"I didn't do anything with my settlement money," Kevin said. "I just left it where it was at. I just kept doing what I was doing. Brenda's lawyers froze all my accounts and I was under court order not to do any spending, so I played by the rules. I was fair, and it cost me. Boy! how it cost me!"

The divorce still took five years, from 1983–88.

"The two lawyers fought and fought and it went out of control," Kevin said. "It was a nightmare."

At one point during the divorce proceedings, one of Brenda's divorce attorneys found Kevin sitting alone in a hallway. Kevin said he got right in his face and whispered, "By the way, I don't give a goddamn if you got money to pay for your medical supplies the rest of your life or not. Where's your lawyer, crip?"

"I didn't say a word to him," Kevin recalled.

"So he says, 'What's the matter? Can't you talk?' Then he gave me a contemptuous little push on the forehead. He just laughed and walked back into the courtroom. I guess that's when the Kansas farm boy finally saw how cruel the world could be."

During the proceedings, Kevin almost immediately went into a period of profound depression. But the divorce wasn't the only nightmare awaiting Kevin. Shortly after word of his $18 million settlement was announced, the little house at 4209 Live Oak became a magnet for every con-artist, crackpot, wild-eyed inventor, entrepreneur, and charity fund-raiser in South Texas.

They found a receptive audience. Kevin suffered through bouts of depression and was still uncomfortable about relying upon others to go anywhere. Most nights he sat home alone and brooded, often with a bottle in his hand. When someone—anyone—would come to visit, even someone wanting money, Kevin was a gracious, attentive host.

"I went through all sorts of investments," Kevin said. "One man wanted $50,000 to develop a self-sanitizing toilet-seat. One company, Gulf Teleport, wanted to build a large satellite dish that would uplink the whole Gulf Coast, from Louisiana to Mexico, and transmit digitally processed information via microwave dishes."

Like most of the others, Gulf Teleport went down the drain. The company needed $17 million, but couldn't arrange interim financing. Kevin lost $45,000 on that one.

"You know, I think these guys think that when it's your money on the line and not their money, they're not really so worried about it if something does or doesn't go," Kevin said. "If I give you $100,000 and you lose it or make something with it, either way it's not really gonna affect your life much, is it?"

Another investment that Kevin was persuaded into making was for an oval race track, a speedway park in Corpus Christi, just like the Daytona 500 track. It was designed for use by race cars, mud racers, 4x4s, everything. They put Kevin on the board of directors to try and make him feel important—to use his money. "I never should have done any of it, but I was looking for a way to feel important again about myself. So, because of my condition, I fell for a lot of things."

Sadly, Kevin never invested in anything that succeeded. When Kevin finally learned his lesson from the speculators, he heeded his family's advice and turned to more legitimate investors. He hired stock brokers to invest in the stock market for him, buying stocks and bonds, and *that* failed. He was losing money instead of making it. It was just disappearing.

Then he invested in real estate, condominiums, and apartment complexes in Texas. But then the bottom fell out of the real estate market in Texas in 1984–85. "You couldn't give 'em away! I had CPAs and lawyers advising me on that one and I *still* ultimately lost $2 or $3 million."

But there was yet *another* way for Kevin to lose money. It was, perhaps, the most insidious, most contemptible of all.

"Sometimes people would come over when I was right out of the hospital and still in a body cast," Kevin said. "They would do little things for me. Some of them were people I really didn't know, but they'd come over and talk with me. They'd say, 'Oh, you need to put a light bulb in there? Let me get a light bulb. Where do you keep your light bulbs? Let me get that.' And they'd sweep up, or pick trash up off the floor like that.

"And afterwards, I'd go, 'You don't have to do that.' And they'd say, 'No, that's okay.' I'd go, 'Well, lemme pay you something.' And they'd say, 'No, no. You don't owe me anything.'

"Then they'd come back two weeks later and they'd want ten, twenty, thirty, forty dollars... or fifty thousand dollars! They'd look at me and say, all hurt-like, 'Well? I helped you out and you're not doing anything and you've got a *lot* of money! All I need is forty thousand dollars—you got millions! What's forty thousand to you?' You do enough of those and you end up with nothing."

There is a quote from David James that Kevin says sums the situation up: "When a person with money meets a person with experience, the person with the money ends up with experience and the person with the experience ends up with the money."

Kevin trusted people. Sometimes they were the wrong people. Sometimes they were friends, guys he went to college with. Sometimes they were professionals. In the end, a lot of them got money from Kevin. And the more he lost, the more depressed he became. Occasionally, he'd try to go out, but would quickly retreat back to his house.

"I hated the way people would look at me funny," he said. "Eventually, I'd just stay home."

For the most part, Kevin's family and friends were helpless to stop the financial bleeding. And there were plenty of sharks around to smell the blood.

"We saw it happening," Freda Saunders said. "We stopped some of it when we went down there from time to time. Once the young man who was working on Kevin's backyard wanted to do it over because he said he wanted a Christmas present for his wife. Donald said, 'The yard doesn't need it.' He said, 'Well, my wife won't get a Christmas present now.' He was mad. But we held firm. Kevin would have just given him more money."

But there were just too many people trying to take advantage of Kevin's position. Everybody wanted his money. And Kevin, not wise to the ways of the world, and battling the effects of loneliness and depression, was easy prey for the ever-present and ever growing school of sharks circling around him, looking for their share of the feeding frenzy.

Then, after the divorce, there wasn't anything left to share.

But Kevin's financial troubles, although grand in scale,

were really secondary compared to the emotional problems that he was struggling with.

"I saw him go through so many different stages," Jack Myers said. "I think one of the saddest times was about two years after he was out, when he was going through all kinds of surgeries. He'd just gotten a motorized cart that enables paraplegics to stand up. At that time he hadn't lifted weights or done anything else athletic since he had been hurt and he had this big ol' pot-belly, no shoulders, no arms to speak of, but he was so proud standing there that I took a picture of him standing there outside his house.

Years later, he showed Kevin the picture, Kevin couldn't believe how bad he looked.

For a while, Jack was very worried about his friend, afraid he would commit suicide, he was so depressed. But all he could do was call, and say, "C'mon Kevin, get out of the house. Get into therapy."

Another problem Kevin had to overcome was the temptation to "party." He had always been a party animal, even back in Downs. Part of that stemmed from the fact that he was never afraid of a dare. He would jump off fifty-foot cliffs because people would dare him to. He couldn't stand being called a "sissy." And this *need* to impress the guys meant he had to prove himself as a real "party animal."

Kevin didn't start drinking until after his junior year in high school. The first drink he ever had was when his best friend Jack Myers got an ID and they drove over to a neighboring town to buy a six-pack. They had two beers each and had to park the car because they couldn't drive home. That was the turning point in Kevin's life when it came to alcohol. Before that, he really didn't want to drink. But once he discovered that he could drink the night before and still do well on the field the next night, then there were no holds barred.

"Especially in high school, I let it get out of hand. I'd come home, hammered to the gills, and get in real trouble with my old man. He'd cuss me out and make me get up at the crack of dawn and do extra chores. He'd stand over me and say, 'You wanna party? Fine. But you damn sure better be ready to get your ass up and get to work!' I don't know if it was good or bad that dad gave me that much lee-way, because I continued to drink a lot for a long time. In junior college, we had players who'd drink Everclear straight! At the time, it seemed to make everything more fun."

But after the accident, Kevin began drinking again to try and forget the fact that he would never walk again—but mostly it was drinking heavily with his rugby buddies. It was a combination of things: being macho, his belief in the old axiom of "work hard—play hard," plus, once Kevin got started at anything, it was hard to stop him. He has always had a tendency to go overboard. So eventually, drinking became something he had to watch very carefully in his life.

"Eventually, though, I realized, probably several years later than I should have, that if you party too much it undoes drastic months of work. And yet, there was always this temptation to party, to forget my situation, to forget reality."

But Kevin's problems had only just begun. The $450,000 house brought on more headaches and, ultimately, more litigation.

"I should have never signed the deal 'cause the builder didn't do what he was supposed to do," Kevin recalled. "He never paid off the subcontractors. It was just a mess all the way around. I ended up being in litigation over that house for many years, mostly with the builder who left town under federal indictment because he messed up a lot of other people besides me."

Kevin then ended up in a grim situation where he allegedly co-signed an additional note for the builder, to keep the builder from defaulting on yet another note. The problem ended up in the lap of a Corpus Christi banker. Kevin eventually ended with a judgment against the bank for more than $40,000, though it was reduced on appeal to $10,000. A flurry of lawsuits and counter-lawsuits with the builder followed. Kevin won a judgment against the builder—as did several sub-contractors—but by then he'd left town and his assets were non-existent.

Meanwhile, the divorce was getting messier—and not coincidentally, more expensive—all the time. Both filed for custody of Steven. The judge, citing both Kevin's status in a wheelchair and the fact that the state traditionally favored the mother regardless of the situation, granted custody to Brenda. The divorce proceedings would last until February 1988—five years later.

"I tried to cope with the stress by having buddies come to visit," Kevin said. "Most of them are real athletic guys and we went out, had fun, did some fun stuff—like riding the off-roaders on the beach.

"After the separation, I got a chance to go date some different girls, too. In fact, they tried to hold that against me in the divorce proceedings. We'd separated and I thought it was time to move on with my life.

"But it ended up costing me again."

Chapter 6

With Kevin spending so much of his time at home, rugby buddy Robert Hays—who was a working carpenter—worked with him to make his house something special. Robert had been a frequent visitor at both the Corpus Christi and Houston hospitals, and often dropped by the house at 4209 Live Oak to keep Kevin company.

"Robert was a real friend; he's always been fair with me," Kevin said. "He's been a friend a long time. Regardless of what happened to me, he's always been straight up. He'd just show up and hang around. If he did work for me, I paid him, period. Just like he can go work anywhere else and get paid, but he knew how much I needed someone to talk to about what had happened. He worked with me, but he also listened a lot."

So, the two of them began working on the house on Live Oak. Kevin liked that house because he had bought it before he was injured. It had many nice features like hardwood floors and such. Kevin and his ex-wife had never really moved in—they were still picking things out when the accident happened—and they had only just planned to move into the house that very weekend.

So Kevin decided to do some renovations before thinking about buying another house. He did some of the planning with Robert while he was still bed-ridden in the hospital.

Over a period of years, the stone house at 4209 Live Oak became something of a showplace. Kevin, Robert, and other friends eventually built a weight room, a sauna, a whirlpool, a steam room, basketball courts, and additional sleeping quarters in the backyard—all connected by wheelchair-friendly ramps. Robert was also one of Kevin's first work-out partners.

"I originally just had one of those big ol' convertible sheds for my weight room," Kevin said, "but we wanted something nicer and somehow the right people came in and it came together at the right time. In time we put a big eight-foot cedar fence all the way around it, so I looked at it like this was a flat in New York City. It doesn't matter who's on your left or right or behind you because you really can't tell anyway. That's the way I built it, with that concept in mind."

Kevin's family and friends took his new-found interest in remodeling the house to be a positive sign and encouraged him to get involved in other activities as well. They reminded him that he couldn't sit around the house forever.

About the same time, Kevin said he also began to get interested in various motivational books. He read them first as a way of coping with the depression and stress resulting from his injury, the divorce, and the multiple lawsuits. Eventually, as he found himself doing more and more interviews and had occasional requests for public speaking, he began to read them for their motivational message and techniques.

"I didn't know it at the time, but those books were slowly convincing me it was time to move on with my life," Kevin said. "There was no one great moment but several smaller events that helped turn me around."

The first such life-changing event occurred in a bar.

At first, Kevin was extremely depressed and didn't want to go out after all that had happened to him, but then, one weekend Robert and some of his other rugby buddies took him to a bar in Houston called Studebaker's.

"I just got inside the front door in my wheelchair and this girl plops in my lap and starts kissing me and making out with me, and she finally got up and I went, 'Where are we?' And they said, 'Studebaker's!' And I said, 'This place is great!'

"I think I realized that night, maybe for the first time, that a guy in a wheelchair can be wanted and liked by other people! You don't have to be on your feet to enjoy life. After my injury, I felt that people didn't really like me—they just used me for the money I'd received in my settlement. That's when I lost some of my trust in people."

Kevin's second life-changing experience was equally by accident.

While he was still in rehab in Houston, there wasn't much talk about wheelchair sports. The therapists seemed resistant to the idea of ordering the new sleek, speedy wheelchairs, preferring instead the standard, hospital wheelchairs. "Maybe they just thought we'd be safer in those chairs," said Kevin. "It's changing now, thank goodness. Many paraplegics now wheel out of the hospital in a state-of-the-art chair.

"I feel that hospitals and therapists handicap their patients even more by putting them in those chairs. When you put people who are already in bad shape in those ancient, awkward chairs, you just make things tougher still. I'd like to put some of those doctors in those chairs and see what *they* think about it."

Kevin's introduction to wheelchair sports came following an anniversary update on survivors of the grain elevator explosion on Corpus Christi television.

The Corpus wheelchair basketball team invited Kevin to play after seeing his interview. He thought it sounded like fun, so eventually he tried it. Some of the guys, like Roland Guzman, Donnie Contrareas, Richard Balli, Joe Garza, and John Finnigan, Kevin got to be good friends with. He felt sure that some of the other guys only wanted him because they thought that, with his millions from the settlement, that he would sponsor the team. But he didn't care.

But first, Kevin decided it was time to get into some kind of physical conditioning.

When he was first released from the hospital, he had a limited range of motion with his body. His arms were very weak. Even lifting a bar with twenty-five pounds on each end was almost impossible for him. It took time to overcome the atrophy in his muscles and get his body into good physical condition. That's why he added the weight room to the house.

"I didn't think there would ever be any kind of athletics in my future. I didn't know they had racing wheelchairs or anything else. They didn't really tell us a lot about those kinds of things at the rehab center."

After working out for some months, Kevin joined the Corpus Christi wheelchair basketball team.

He discovered that most of those guys on the wheelchair team weren't in tremendous shape, either. Most of them were overweight. Kevin was competitive even in his hospital chair. He found that he could move and be productive in that wheelchair basketball setting, it just wasn't much exercise.

Although Kevin quickly became an important member of the team, the old will to win wasn't really present. Between games, he'd continue his long bouts with depression, punctuated by occasional lost weekends where the parties and alcohol blotted out the pain—and memories.

Among those who were worried about Kevin were his brother Gerald and his family. Gerald had established a thriving accounting business in South Carolina. But the family always drove to Atlanta to compete in the Peachtree Road Race 10K.

"We'd run the year before and that's when we saw the wheelchair division," Gerald said. "That was at the beginning of it—of course, back then it wasn't as crowded as it is now. So we thought, 'Hey, maybe this is something Kevin can compete in because he loves to compete.'" Gerald and his wife Verla thought that maybe it would be beneficial for Kevin to get in there and compete, because it was something he could actually do and achieve in a wheelchair and, by doing that, pick up his spirits and give him the desire to get back to the competition he enjoyed before the accident. And that would give him a better life.

Gerald's invitation to come to Simpsonville, South Carolina, visit the family, and, coincidentally, run in the Peachtree was issued in June 1983.

Kevin decided to "go for it" even though he knew he

wasn't really in any kind of shape, but thought he could do it because of his basketball playing. After all, he had been an athlete before the explosion and he figured this "wheelchair stuff couldn't be all that hard!" And Kevin had always been able to take on any kind of challenge before. How far could the finish line be?

The flight to Atlanta was Kevin's first major trip after his accident. He went partly because Gerald asked, and partly because the whole idea of a wheelchair race intrigued him. So he just dropped everything and went out there, not knowing how long the Peachtree was—not knowing anything about racing at all. "I just went because Gerald asked me. It just sounded like fun to me."

But when the race actually began, Kevin discovered that he was totally unprepared. He had no gloves, no hand tape, no water—none of the essentials. When the other wheelchair racers saw him, they said, "You better get in your racer, it's almost time for the race to start." He looked at them and said, "I'm already in it." They just laughed.

When the starting gun fired, Kevin looked up and the other racers were gone, long gone. Still, Kevin says he was hooked, almost from the first few minutes of the race.

The raceway was packed with people on the sidelines and they were cheering all the way. Kevin found the experience exhilarating, especially when he got going downhill and went flying down the road.

"My hands got all blistered by mile four. I looked up at mile four and there was this hill. To me it looked a mile long and about a forty-five degree angle. Actually, it was probably only a 1/2 to 3/4 mile long and about a thirty-three degree angle. There was a sign at the bottom of the hill that said 'Cardiac Hill.' I looked at my hands and I looked at the hill again and I said, 'No way, I ain't going.'

"But everybody gets to the bottom of the hill at one time or another. If you're in school, it might be a math test, it might be a PE class, it might be something that happens to you on the way to school. You might have something happen to you in life that makes you feel you can't get over it. Everyone needs a little motivation, a pat on the back, or a hug, or you need to see something or hear something supportive.

"And for me that day was something I heard in my head, it was 'Dunh-ditty-dunh-ditty-dunh—dunh dunnnhhh!'—the *Rocky* movies' theme music."

The next few minutes were among the most agonizing of Kevin's life. With his bare hands, both bloody and peeling, he began to methodically pull himself up Cardiac Hill. The blood from the broken blisters caused his hands to slip on more than one occasion and he'd slide helplessly backwards for several feet until he could dry his hands and try again.

Muscles in his arms and back—muscles that hadn't been used since before the accident—screamed in protest. Kevin bit through his lip in determination and pain. He was afraid to release his grip on the wheels to wipe the sweat from his face because he'd lose precious ground once again.

The encouraging roar of the crowd lining the hill became like white noise, filling in the background. Kevin cried audibly with each pull. Life narrowed to a spearpoint, to a single action, to a single pull of the wheels. And when that motion was completed, he thought about the single action to come: the next painful, methodical, wrenching pull on the wheelchair's slippery wheels.

Suddenly, the hill was no more.

"I just cranked that old hospital chair over the top of that hill. For the first time since my accident, I felt a sense of accomplishment. It felt great!" Kevin said. "And I only had a mile to go to the finish line and that was all downhill. When I hear that *Rocky* music, something comes over me. I feel like I'm Rocky training for that big fight. That music really gives me an incredible high. You can overcome impossible odds. You feel like you're indestructible. And for a moment, I did. I felt indestructible again.

"I was nearly dead, but I said, 'Man, I'm gonna make it to the finish line! I got a mile to go and it's downhill. I can coast most of it!'"

But the Peachtree, like many road races of its day, had a hard-fast rule in events where there are tens of thousands of participants. If a foot runner passes a wheelchair athlete—the wheelchair event begins thirty minutes earlier—then the wheelchair athlete must leave the course immediately. For safety reasons, of course.

At the very top Kevin was passed by a foot runner. Suddenly, a very large woman with a 'Race Official' t-shirt came off the side of Peachtree Street, grabbed him by the shoulder and said, "You've got to get off now, you've been passed by a foot runner."

"I just turned around to her and said, 'No way, lady! I've come this far and I'm not stopping now!' And I pushed loose from her and I was gonna make it to the finish line! So I started pumping again. But she got three more race officials that looked just like her and they set a roadblock in the road that I couldn't get around.

"Those four big ol' ladies physically pulled me off the race course that day. I tried to fight them off, but I couldn't in the old hospital chair. I was mad and sad all at one time. I was crying. It was the lowest moment of my life. I could feel the people along the road staring at me, some of them were laughing, some of them felt sorry for me.

"I'd always been an athlete, I'd always been good at any kind of athletic endeavors. I thought I was going to make it, and to get up there and not even make it, I was so humiliated. It may sound stupid for a guy who never ran anything in a wheelchair to feel that way, but I felt somehow I should have been able to overcome it. I gave it all I had, I just couldn't make it. They wouldn't let me. You just can't imagine. I'd poured my heart and soul out into a race like that, yet they didn't care. I wheeled myself onto a side street and just sat there."

Gerald was running in that same race and since the wheelchair runners began way ahead of the regular runners, he didn't think to look for Kevin when he passed him on the course. But when he got to the end of the race, one of his sons explained to him what had happened. They walked back to where he was at and brought him to the finish. He was still very upset about being pulled out of the race.

But somewhere on Cardiac Hill, something had changed.

After the onlookers had thinned out following the conclusion of the race, Kevin found himself alone. And self-pity turned, somehow, into resolve.

"I think that suddenly, at that moment, I realized I'd been depending on other people: my doctors, my therapists, my friends, and my family. I was dependent on others for who I was and where I was going. I realized if I was going to get anywhere in life, it was going to be up to me."

When those race officials dragged Kevin from the race, they hadn't understood what he had been trying to achieve, that he had worked so hard. It had taken everything he had to get as far as he did.

"But rules are rules, and some people, give them a little authority and they will take it all the way. Those women fought like tigers to get me off the road, like it was their job, their duty, their life's call. They had to strip me from that road race, but they did more than that: they stripped me of my dignity and pride. I hardly ever cry, but that day... sometimes some things just bring tears to your eyes.

Kevin doesn't like to think about what happened at the top of that hill that day because he still feels the humiliation, the hot, shameful tears coming to his eyes and the sadness he felt facing his family, knowing that he never made it to the finish line. But that day Kevin made a decision. He decided to take action, to do something, to get somewhere.

"I set a goal that day: I never wanted to let that happen to me again in my life. I'd never be pulled from a race like that again. No one would control my destiny ever again.

"I also realized, maybe for the first time, that while there was a million things I could do on my feet, there was still *nine hundred and ninety-nine thousand* things I could do in my chair! I decided to quit focusing on the thousand things I couldn't do."

Gerald said the change in the Kevin he found on the side of Peachtree Street startled him.

"Even then, I could tell he was serious about finishing the rest of the race," Gerald said. "He immediately went home and ordered a running chair. It was obvious he was hooked on it and he was going to beat it."

When Kevin returned from Atlanta, a book was waiting. It was a gift from George Raveling, then head basketball coach at Washington State. Coach Raveling had heard about Kevin's accident and sent him a copy of *Yes, You Can!*, Art Linkletter's biography.

It tells about how Art left home with ten dollars sewed in his jacket when he was sixteen years old and how he went on to become a multimillionaire. It also explains how he views life, how he treats other people, and what his work ethic is. But just as important as the book, was a letter that Coach Raveling included in the book, urging Kevin to carry on, to work towards his greatest potential.

When Kevin returned home, he ordered a racing wheelchair and started talking to wheelchair athletes like George Murray, Randy Snow, Mike Trujillo, Marty Ball, Phil Carpenter, Bob Gibson, Marty Mourse, Rafael Ibarra, and Greg Gibbens. He talked to local coaches, like Gerald Rodriguez, a junior high coach in Corpus Christi nicknamed "Rocky." He asked some of his old friends like Jack Myers—just to get ideas about what they thought he should do.

He started to find out how to train, what to eat. He went to a high school track to practice and went out on the streets. There was a lot of trial and error in the beginning, and it was a constant learning process.

Among Kevin's early heroes was David Wear, an Austin, Texas, native, who had excelled in the first national wheelchair competition in both track and field events and weightlifting. Another hero was George Murray, the first disabled athlete to be featured on a Wheaties box, after being named amateur athlete of the year in 1978. They sold something like four million boxes of Wheaties with his picture on the cover.

What really caught Kevin's attention was a photograph of Randy Snow, of Dallas, accepting the silver medal on the winner's stand at the Olympics. It was in an article in *Sports and Spokes* magazine about racing in the Olympic stadium. Kevin decided he wanted to do something like that. He wanted to be in a wheelchair and still have the opportunity to win an Olympic medal—until then, he hadn't even known there were wheelchair events in the Olympics.

Thinking back, he realized that all of his best friends from high school, college, even after college, were athletes. And he wanted to get back into that environment.

Kevin tracked down Randy at various Texas track meets and tennis matches, made his acquaintance, and soon the two became friends.

At the time, Randy Snow was one of America's best-known paraplegic athletes. While working on a farm in 1975, a thousand-pound bale of hay fell on him from a lift, crushing his spinal cord. From then on, Randy's career was a roller-coaster ride of athletic highs and alcohol- and drug-induced lows. As a wheelchair tennis player, he won the U.S. Open men's singles nine times. Before earning the silver medal in the 1,500 meters at the Los Angeles Olympics in 1984, he trained for a year at the University of Houston with Carl Lewis' coach, Tom Tellez. Similar ups and downs followed in the years ahead.

But sensing a kindred spirit in Kevin, the two almost immediately began working together.

"When Kevin first got hurt, he was real interested in a lot of different wheelchair sports," Randy said. "He swam, bowled, shot rifles, played basketball, he did everything. And that's usually what happens. After someone gets hurt, they're real negative for a while. Then they're exposed to different sports and they just kind of dive in—want to do everything. Then, as time goes on, they figure out what they really enjoy doing. That's how Kevin got to Barcelona."

Randy's new-found notoriety attracted a number of people in the days following the Summer Olympics, including a number of wheelchair athletes. Randy said he acknowledged everybody, but waited to see who was serious.

"I remember Kevin having a real passion for the sports and recreation," Randy said. "I thought he would stick around because he was real eager and got involved early after the rehab process.

"I kept training, and Kevin would sometimes come and push with us. He was real green at that time. He had a lot of energy, was real motivated, he just wasn't very good at it yet. It takes a lot of time, you can't just do it in a year or two—it takes a lot of years."

Both Randy and Kevin point to the wheelchair 1,500 meters in the Summer Games as a pivotal point in the history of wheelchair athletics.

"Wheelchair athletics had existed before then—we go all of the way back to the fifties and sixties," Randy said. "But the acceptance level at that time wasn't very high. The Olympics were the first time the highest governing body of sports on the planet for able-bodied individuals looked in our direction and acknowledged wheelchair athletes.

"They said, by letting us compete there, that 'We realize that you're not mentally handicapped. This is a not a Special Olympics event. We acknowledge that you are athletes and we will allow you to compete in the Olympics.' It was the first time that had ever happened. So it was very pivotal. The competition was in Los Angeles and was aired live across the world. When we wheeled on the track, everybody just looked. They'd heard of wheelchair events, but they didn't know what was going on. And then when we ran a 1,500 meters in less than four minutes, they were blown away."

In time, Kevin felt comfortable enough to invite Randy to a party at his house in Corpus Christi. Randy came, brought his medal, and told Kevin all about it. Kevin also learned about the upcoming Paralympic Games in Seoul, Korea, in 1988, and told Randy, "I wanna go for it."

The party went well. Many people there couldn't believe

that a person in a wheelchair could win an Olympic medal. But there it was! "That kind of hurt my feelings for some reason. It didn't bother Randy. He said, 'That's fine, you don't have to believe it.' He told me, 'It's OK, they wouldn't appreciate it anyway.' And he put it up.

"But I never forgot it. Even if all the people milling around, drinking and laughing didn't appreciate what it had cost Randy—I did. Winning a medal in a wheelchair is as great an accomplishment as an able-bodied person winning a medal—maybe greater when you consider *what* put someone in that chair. Besides that, competing in the Olympics is something a lot of us in wheelchairs thought we'd never have."

Later that same evening, one of the party-goers walked up to Randy and Kevin, stared at them for a moment, and said, "Hey, are you guys in some kind of health club or something? You don't look like normal wheelchair guys. You're, like, bulked up and in good shape."

Randy laughed it off, but the comment profoundly affected Kevin. No one had ever said that to him before. And he liked hearing it.

"It was an important night for me," Kevin said. "After everybody left, Randy and I talked a long time. He's my friend and I was happy for his success. I'm just not the jealous type. Instead, hanging out with someone like Randy makes me think some of it is going to rub off on me! Not that I'd ever want to take away from Randy's or anybody's accomplishments, but it gives me something to work towards."

The next day, Kevin began training seriously on his own. He began doing long, long workouts on the track, workouts in the weight room, and cranking the rollers and dips and chins. In a year or so, he was doing 250 chins and a thousand dips a day.

Then he began practicing each day at Moody High School track in Corpus. In the beginning, he was only doing about forty miles around the track in his chair and only lifted weights twice a week. He could push about ten kilometers in about forty minutes. And to train for the slopes and hills in the races, he practiced on the grassy sides of the expressway near his house.

"And I had one goal in mind. I put up a sign in my bedroom that said, '1988 medalist, Seoul Korea.' I looked at it every day."

It didn't happen right away of course, but in time Kevin discovered that he wanted to do everything possible to achieve that goal. He realized that the amount of focus and effort you put into something really pays off in the end. You get out of life what you put into it. He knew what he had to do.

Needless to say, this change in Kevin was welcomed by his family and friends—though even they didn't realize how profound that change was or how far it would take him.

As the various championship competitions began to near, Kevin realized that training on his own in Corpus Christi wasn't enough. He made inquiries and decided to train—at least part time—with other athletes in Houston in 1984. The rest of the time he trained with Gerald "Rocky" Rodriquez, a junior high school football and track coach. "Rocky" and Kevin left every morning before dawn to train on the access road. One morning a semi-truck didn't see the two men and nearly decapitated Kevin.

"What you think is training hard and what training hard is with other top athletes are two completely different things," Kevin said. "You think you've done your best while you're on your own—until you start working out and against someone else who is in slightly better shape. It makes you better. Still, it took me a while to adjust to that.

The Southwest Wheelchair Athletic coach, Judy Einbinder, the Olympic liaison for the disabled athletes, found Kevin to be a challenging, sometimes infuriating, pupil. Einbinder first became involved with wheelchair sports more than a decade ago and was instrumental in organizing the first wheelchair race exhibition in Los Angeles in 1984, and was also a pivotal figure in the aligning of the Paralympics with the regular Olympics.

"I've got a reputation with our athletes that I don't exactly treat them with kid gloves. We're trying to achieve athletic excellence. There are other people who can deal with the other stuff going on in their lives. My job is to prepare them for competition to the best of my ability. It took a while for Kevin adapt to that."

Kevin would train in Houston with several athletes, then return to Corpus Christi to train on his own and—partly—to get his confidence back up. He wasn't used to Einbinder's Marine Boot Camp-styled discipline.

"I was trying to get back in good health in the beginning," he said. "I was in pretty poor shape. It wasn't so bad going around town, but it's totally different than actually getting out and cranking around the track. Most people don't understand what physical effort it takes for track and field.

"But I found that pain alone wasn't going to stop me. Pain's the goal. That's how you get stronger, faster, quicker, sharper. To excel in athletics, there has to be pain to get to that point."

With that realization, Kevin discovered that, for someone with his goals, wheelchair basketball was not the ideal sport.

He found that the amount of physical effort involved was dependent too much upon his fellow teammates (for example, how often they would pass him the ball). He preferred the more individual challenge of track and field where his success was completely dependent upon his own commitment, sacrifice, and focus.

Kevin stuck with basketball anyway, and eventually was named Outstanding Athlete in the Lone Star Basketball Conference for 1984. The league consisted of Austin, San Antonio, McAllen, Corpus Christi, and Houston.

Kevin played on the Corpus Christi team in Class I. The event was divided it into three classes, which were determined by level of disability. Kevin was in the class with the highest level of injury. Those in class II had more control over their bodies, and those in Class III could walk.

"We had a lot of good players, but we didn't play team basketball—it was every man for himself. We didn't have any offensive plays. Some guys would play man to man, others would play a zone—at the same time. It was like street ball. So the next year I decided to move on to track and field exclusively and let basketball go."

After more than a year of work, Kevin finally felt confident enough to enter his first track meet, the Ninth Annual Southwest Wheelchair Athletic Association Regional Games in Houston. In the Games, which were held in April 1984, Kevin entered the pentathlon for the first time and took home the bronze medal. He also won gold medals in the javelin, bowling, and the middle-weight class weightlifting, and silver medals in the shot put and discus.

"I did OK for being a novice competitor," Kevin said. "And I learned that after only a year of serious training I could medal with guys who'd been doing it for years."

It was about this time that Terry Jessup entered Kevin's life. Terry had been a track and field coach on the club level in the Dallas area since the early 1960s. In early 1984, the Southwest Wheelchair Association's coach urged him to get involved in wheelchair athletics as well.

His early impressions of Kevin were that he was talented, but that he was not packaged well, meaning that his strategies for training and competing needed better planning and more focus.

Still, Kevin's performances in Houston and other meets enabled him to enter the National Wheelchair Track and Field Championships, held near Johnson City, Tennessee, at East Tennessee State in May of 1984.

"I got a bronze medal in the pentathlon," Kevin said. "That was a big deal for me, to see all the best guys in the U.S. and to actually win a bronze medal. I did it by the skin of my teeth; I barely got in there. I had to make a certain score in the 1,500 meters to squeeze into third, and that's what I did. Some of the guys who could have beaten me fouled out early, but I still hung on and made it. That's what it takes to get in the door. That win gave me more self-esteem than anything I'd done up to that point.

"That's probably one of my favorite medals. It was the first one I won in a national championship. It said 'USA' on the medal—I was really proud of that, mostly because I was still learning, still building myself up."

Not that the win came easily. Kevin said he found many of the top wheelchair athletes aloof and distant—and sometimes downright rude.

"Nobody gave me much attention or talked to me very much. It was like a closed circle, where the better you were, the more other people would recognize you and talk to you."

Randy Snow agreed, at least in the early days, that wheelchair athletes were a cliquish, sometimes elitist group. He attributes much of the aloof attitude to the intensely competitive nature of the sport.

"Me, I just love people and Kevin was from Texas and when I get into national and international competitions, I just hang out with my fellow Texans. I'm proud of them. I remember Kevin from that meet. I remember even thinking, 'I wonder if he's going to make it?'"

Even through the snubs and sneers, Kevin still counts the meet at Johnson City, Tennessee, as one of the highlights of his competitive life.

"The meet was pretty overwhelming," he said. "Just to be there, to live in a dormitory was something, especially as a rookie. I had never experienced any of that before. But just being at East Tennessee was even more amazing. I saw the guys from the Olympic trial race for the 1984 Olympics. I got to see Randy Snow, Jim Martinsen and Jim Knaub and Jimmy Green and George Murray, all those guys ran that race. It was real exciting to see how fast they went.

"I felt privileged to be there and visit with them. And, as I did, I thought of all the millions of disabled people who never made it, who were never able to take a step, to get out and do anything like that to be around those kind of people.

"I think the people who *are* out there stretching themselves and doing things in life are going to find life a lot more enjoyable and fulfilling than those people who sit around and do nothing. Most people don't want to stretch themselves, they don't want to get outside their comfort zone. After Tennessee, I could never go back to that."

Despite his exceptional medal haul, Kevin knew that his times and distances still weren't good enough to get him to Seoul.

"It takes time to adjust to your new body, and to learn to make it work for you—only in a different way. There are different exercises, different movements than you are used to than when you had the use of your legs."

Kevin returned to Corpus Christi and not only continued his training regimen, he attacked it with renewed vigor. On July 4, 1984, he returned to Atlanta for his second Peachtree. Only this time, he came in a sleek new racing chair, armed with the latest equipment and clothing, including a tank shirt with a Texas flag on the front. After only a year of training, he finished twenty-first in the wheelchair division. And no race stewards kept him from the finish line.

In December of 1984, Kevin was involved in a fund-raiser for the Therapeutic Recreation Section of the Corpus Christi Parks and Recreation Service. Along with other members of the Corpus Christi Wheelchair Basketball Team, Kevin wheeled himself 150 miles from San Antonio to Corpus. The money he raised through pledges went to the Therapeutic Recreation Section.

In 1985, Kevin competed in a number of major wheelchair events, including the national track and field meet in Edinboro, Pennsylvania, the National Wheelchair Games, and the 1985 Strohs Run for Liberty—where he ran the fastest time in the nation with a 21:07 in the 8K.

After one such race, Kevin told reporter Buck Francis that he wasn't just training and racing for himself—he had a larger mission in mind: "One of the reasons I'm furthering my athletic career is to prove to other handicapped persons that you don't have to give up being active just because you're disabled. I want to project a positive image to handicapped people."

In October 1985, Kevin donated the money to Downs High School that would enable the school to build a track and field facility. The athletes had previously been forced to train on a well-rutted dirt path around the football field that was only usable a few days during the rainy spring season.

Kevin was honored at half time of the football game, along with several others, at Dillon Field, "Home of the Dragons." In addition to the track, Kevin made other donations to DHS for computer and video equipment for the grade school and shop equipment for the high school.

As he told *The Downs News* that day: "I believe anyone can do anything if they work hard enough and I think this track might be the difference in a state competition championship."

Kevin's words proved prophetic. In 1989, four years after the donation of what was officially named "Saunders Track," those seniors who were freshmen in 1984 led the school to the Kansas high school state championship for the first time since the 1930s.

"That makes you feel good, knowing you are part of making a dream come true for something like that," he said. "Of course, that was back when I still had some money."

Back on the wheelchair athletics circuit, as Kevin began to prosper in the meets, he became a popular focus of the local media. And when they weren't interviewing Kevin, they were interviewing Kevin's teammates *about* Kevin.

Bruce Acuna, a member of the Corpus Christi Rugby Club who competed with Kevin before the accident, and who later often accompanied him to track meets, told writer Diane Gasper-O'Brien that Kevin was still an encouragement to the rugby team.

"He's been a good inspiration to us," Bruce said. "If somebody gives him a challenge, he'll meet it head on.

"We work out a lot together, and if we drag around, he'll tell us, 'If I was on my feet, I'd give it all I had.' If you don't want to work and instead just sit around, he doesn't want to be around you. If you want to hang around him, you'd better to ready for something to happen."

Bruce was right: sometimes things just *happened* when Saunders was around. About this time, Saunders was dating a beautiful young lady from Venezuela. After a meet in San Antonio on Friday night, he went with some friends to a well-known bar in the Alamo City.

"Some guys there were really rude to us," Kevin recalled. "I'd try to pass by them saying, 'excuse me' because of the wheelchair and these guys would say 'Screw you, go around.' I said, 'Okay, no problem, I'll go around,'" Kevin, who wasn't looking to cause any trouble, finally left with his friend Dr. Oran Burnett, M.D. When they got to the hotel, Kevin called a friend, who was living in Houston at the time, told her what had happened, and asked her to fly to San Antonio and bring some nice clothes—especially a miniskirt.

When she arrived Saturday night, they all went back to the same club, but Kevin went in separately from his girlfriend. He asked her to stand right around the dance floor and not to talk to anybody or dance with anybody. After a while, he would come up from time to time and ask her to dance. When people asked her why she was dancing with a guy in a wheelchair and nobody else, she'd say, "Because he looks good."

This went on all evening until Kevin and his girlfriend became inseparable. The entire scene was played out in front of the same rude young men from the previous night.

"All night, those guys were breathing down her neck, and boy! were they pissed!" Kevin recalled. "I kept getting a little closer and closer to her, and she ended up sitting in my lap and giving me hugs and little kisses. By now, these guys were just fuming.

"I'll never forget the looks on their faces when it was obvious that she was leaving with me."

In June 1985, Kevin was selected to compete in the International Wheelchair Games in Adelaide, South Australia, Jan. 18–28, 1986. Kevin was accompanied by

Robert Hays. In addition to the pentathlon, Kevin competed in the pistol, the javelin, and the 200-meter dash.

The competition was held on an old cinder track not far from the hotel where Kevin and Robert were staying. While Kevin was practicing, he had problems with his field chair. When the Australian wheelchair athletes, who were also practicing, saw that Kevin was having troubles, one of them loaned him his field chair! "That's pretty unusual when you are competing against people," said Kevin. "On that day, not only did I win the pentathlon with a then-world record point total of 3,771, I beat Bruce Waldrip, the world record holder in the javelin and discus, in the javelin as well—and won another gold medal!

"I was crazy about Australia: a lot of beautiful women, a lot of friendly people, great music in all of the pubs— they even had a big gambling casino. There were so many things to see and do, Robert and I decided to stay over and check the country out in a rented Winnebago!

"The thing I remember most about Australia, more than the Opera House or the natural beauty, was that when we'd go into a pub, there were always three girls for every guy! It was like paradise! Robert said if he ever came back, he'd never leave."

After a silver medal in the pentathlon at the 28th National Wheelchair Games in Edinboro, Pennsylvania in July 1985, Kevin decided to skip most of the wheelchair track and field competitions in 1986. The governing body of the wheelchair athletics association decided to split the track and field events among several different sites—which were then held at different times during the year. However, when they didn't draw a big crowd of athletes that year, the association went back to the old format.

Kevin concentrated on road races, particularly 10Ks. But as the Paralympic Games in Seoul loomed, Kevin decided to return to track and field competition in late 1986.

It was about this time that Kevin met the athlete who was to become his closest rival over the next few years, William Brady.

William either owns or has owned the U.S. records in the shot put, javelin, and discus since the beginning of serious track and field competition in the early 1980s, following a motorcycle accident that left him a paraplegic in 1979. One of his early goals when he started competition was to break all existing U.S. track and field records. In time, he accomplished exactly that.

A design engineer in nuclear services for Duke Power in North Carolina, William is the rare world-class wheelchair athlete with a family and a full-time job. Somehow, he has managed to win more than forty gold, silver, and bronze medals in national and international competition and keep both his family *and* his job. William's fierce determination, particularly in the field events, is legendary in the sport.

"From our first meet, I think I saw that Kevin had a burning desire to be on top and that's what it takes in a competitive athlete," William said. "You've got to have that desire and motivation within yourself to go through all of the drudgery and all the training. For myself, I really don't enjoy that. I enjoy the competition, representing my country, wearing the U.S.A. uniform in front of sixty thousand people, and all of the newspaper articles—there's a lot of pride there, there's a lot of pride in being an American. But not the training and the hours."

William says that both of them were intensely competitive long before fate put them in wheelchairs.

"I think those things kind of carry over," he said. "Just because you become disabled and you're competing in a wheelchair, if you have that competitiveness in yourself, it doesn't go away. And when you get into international competitions and world records and the Olympics—it just intensifies it.

"One thing Kevin and I have in common is that burning desire to be #1. It's not over that little piece of metal; the piece of metal you could probably buy in a store somewhere for a few bucks. That's just kind of symbol of what you're really after—and that's to be the best you can really be."

One of the most important meets for Kevin was the 30th Annual National Wheelchair Games in Houston in the middle of June, 1987.

He was still holding the world record in the pentathlon at the time, and was also competing in the 200-, 400-, 800-, and 1,500- meter runs, various pistol and rifle divisions, *and* weightlifting. His main goal was to secure a spot in Seoul, Korea, in the pentathlon for the 1988 Paralympic Games. At that time, his best time in the 1,500 meters was 4:07.

By 1987, Kevin was in the pack with some of the faster runners, in the thick of the action. All of a sudden, wheelchair athletes who were famous all across the country started to know who Kevin was.

As the race for the three pentathlon spots on the U.S. Paralympic Team in Seoul intensified, three athletes began to pull away from the field: Doug Kennedy, William Brady and Kevin Saunders. At one meet, only eight points out of nearly four thousand possible points separated the three competitors.

Unfortunately for Kevin, there was more to life than training and competing in track meets. In 1987, his divorce proceedings were winding down, but they remained acrimonious and distracting. The various litigation involving the grain elevator explosion was continuing as well. More than once, Kevin was called away from training to testify in court.

Even so, when the U.S. Paralympic Trials were finally held in Edinboro, Pennsylvania in June 1988, Kevin qualified—and was as ready as he'd ever been. When the dust settled, he'd won the silver medal in the pentathlon and earned a trip to Seoul, along with William and Doug Kennedy. But more surprising, he qualified in the discus, shot put, and javelin, as well as the 200 meters.

Not that life went smoothly after the Trials, either.

He found out after the Trials in June that he would have to get a chair without steering. For someone in a wheelchair, that was a major adjustment.

Kevin's original chair was like a bicycle—he was able

to steer it around the track. But his new chair would feel to Kevin like someone had welded the handle bars and the front wheels together. So the chair would only roll straight.

But finally, about three weeks before the Games, he found a chair without steering that he felt comfortable with, made by Bobby Hall, the first wheelchair racer to win the Boston Marathon. He now owns a wheelchair manufacturing company called Halls Wheels in Massachusetts. Everything was starting to click.

Chapter 7

The announcement that Kevin had made the U.S. Paralympic Team and would be competing in Seoul, Korea, caught even some of his closest friends and family members by surprise.

Jack Myers said: "I'd see him do great at some meets, then after some meets he'd go out and drink beer. It really didn't make sense. But then, I really wasn't around day in and day out, meet to meet. But he kept getting more confident and more confident and more serious and more serious and the better he got, the more seriously he took it. "

Duane Saunders said initially he wasn't sure that Kevin was *really* getting to go.

"At first, I had to filter it out some," Duane said. "Is he really doing this? Or is he blowing smoke? But when he really qualified, I knew I had to go. I thought heck, let's just do it. I fly so much, I've got more frequent flier tickets than I'll ever use. So I called Gerald and said, 'Do you want to go to Seoul? We should take dad'—who was then seventy-nine years old. We also decided to take my son Don, who was twelve. I told Gerald if he'd help out with the hotel bill, I'd spring for the four airplane tickets to Seoul. We did it. They all came up to Minneapolis so we could fly out together.

"My dad was ready to go, then he got worried if he could go to the bathroom on the airplane! He almost backed out a week before, but we forced him at the last minute to go. He was still worried about the bathrooms, even in the air on the 757. Turns out, his seat was in the last row—next to the bathroom!

"We laughed the whole ten days in Seoul. When Grandpa Saunders went to the shopping places in Seoul, the Koreans would make a big deal: 'Grandfather, father, son. How old are you?' 'I'll be eighty years old next year,' he'd say. They had a fit over him. Eventually, if we went into a shop and they *didn't* ask him how old he was, Grandpa Saunders went up and told them."

"It *was* a lot of fun," Jack Myers said. "I remember getting goose bumps just walking into the stadium. When I arrived, I hadn't seen Kevin yet because we flew in three to four days after he did. I got a schedule of his events and went to the stadium and there he was out on the field. It was a big thrill.

"To be in a situation like that, coming from a small town like we did, it was a little overwhelming to actually believe I was sitting there watching a friend compete in the Olympics—I was never so proud in my life. I'm proud to this day to tell people I know him. He's still an inspiration to me. What little problems I have are nothing compared to what he's been through."

First staged in Rome in 1960, the Paralympics have been held in the host country of the able-bodied Olympics every year except 1968 (Israel) and 1980 (Holland). More than four thousand athletes and staff traveled to Seoul from October 15–24, 1988. The Seoul Paralympic Organizing committee and the Korean people raised 23 billion *won* to stage the games. Before it was over, the Seoul Paralympics drew more spectators than Toronto (1976), Arnhem (1980), and Nassau (1984) combined.

International Olympic Committee President Juan Antonio Samarach opened the ceremonies. After his visit to Seoul, Samarach made the following statement: "...the Games provided a turning point in the growing sports for the disabled movement. Through the VII Paralympic Games, sports for the handicapped gained greater recognition and acceptance by society in general and are, indeed, coming to be viewed as legitimate sports in their own right."

The Seoul Games marked the first time there was a unified American contingent. Under the leadership of the United States Olympic Committee's Committee on Sport for the Disabled, the U.S. Disabled Sports Team (USDST) totaled 495 individuals—which included 376 athletes. It also marked the first Paralympic Games in which athletes from the then-Soviet Union were allowed to participate.

The Paralympics were held at several different venues: the Seoul Sports Complex, Olympic Park, Sangmu Sport Complex, and the Chung-Nip Polio Center.

"It was a great honor to go over to Seoul and represent my country," Kevin recalled. "It was an incredible high to be down there on the Olympic Stadium track and in the gigantic stadium and be staying in the Olympic Village. I really felt like I had accomplished something."

The opening ceremonies went like clockwork: impressive, dazzling in their size and beauty, awe-inspiring in their precision. Unfortunately, nothing in the Seoul Paralympics would work as smoothly again.

"I kept asking, 'Where do we report for the [200-meter] race?'" Kevin said, "but nobody spoke English and I never could get an answer from anybody. Suddenly, I discovered that the entries were closed and I was scratched!"

Kevin was not alone in his confusion. Mary Margaret "Boodie" Newsom, manager of Library & Education Services for the United States Olympic Committee in Colorado Springs, Colorado, who was the *Chef de Mission* to Seoul, later said her greatest disappointment was the last-minute cancellation of two hundred events from the schedule, affecting eighty athletes. Most switched to other events, even though they hadn't been training in those events, and four athletes were unable to compete at all.

Not only that, but a final competition schedule, listing all events, was not distributed until the end of the Games—when it was no longer useful. Therefore, athletes and coaches never had a comprehensive schedule, nor did parents, media or others who needed to know what was scheduled to happen when.

Daily schedules were made and distributed each evening for the next day's competition, but these were always subject to change—Newsom received more than a few calls in the wee hours of the morning telling her that an event time or start order had been changed, and that she was responsible for notifying the coaches and athletes involved. In some sports, such as swimming, there were on some days no start lists distributed before events, so all athletes had to get up early and go to the venue, not knowing if and when they would have to compete.

When the time finally came for the pentathlon, the five events were spread over two days. The pentathlon started badly for Kevin.

"My shot put was terrible," he said. "Doug Kennedy, from Alabama, and I got red-flagged on some of our throws so we only got one throw in each and mine was very substandard."

Then it was time for the javelin. William 'Bubba' Brady, Doug Kennedy, and Kevin are arch rivals. When Brady threw the javelin, it headed toward some steel markers. It came down tail-first, which is a no-throw, but somehow the tail hit the big metal marker, flew up, and went about another ten to twelve feet on down the field. The referee didn't see it and marked it! Doug looked over at Kevin as if to say "Can you believe a stroke of luck like that?"

"After that, it looked like Brady was the only American guy in contention for a medal. Doug was plumb out of the medal competition. Still, Doug and I had a good 200-meter race. After that, there was German in first place, a Finn in second, and Brady was third."

But Kevin had an exceptional throw in the discus that moved him up several positions. Doug, alas, didn't do as well, throwing what the other athletes called a "dying quail."

That set up the 1,500 meters as the decisive event—as it is in most pentathlons.

"Doug was real fast on the track," Kevin said. "He's a sub-3:45 1,500 meter guy—a real speed demon. They told me if I beat Brady by fifty seconds, there was a good chance I might nip him out of the bronze medal slot. I didn't have a chance to beat the silver or gold guys."

Doug decided that he would draft Kevin.

Kevin laughed at the suggestion—but Doug was deadly serious.

"Wind blocking" or "drafting" is a controversial race tactic in wheelchair sports. In it, a lead wheelchair both creates a "draft" that pulls the second chair along *and* blocks the wind for the second chair.

So Doug blocked the wind for Kevin, and when the race was over, Kevin had beaten Brady by fifty-three seconds—and twenty-six points, finishing with a total of 3046.885 points.

U.S. coach Judy Einbinder said the rivalry among William, Doug, and Kevin has resulted in some memorable pentathlons in recent years—though none more heated than at Seoul that day.

"If Brady could get his act together on the track and train full time, Kevin would be in big trouble," said Einbinder. "But he just can't do it with a full-time job and a family. And pushing 1,500 meters you have to train every day. You have to get mileage in, you have to get speed work in, and you've got to know a little bit about the strategy and tactics of wheelchair racing. Brady trains on his own, whereas Kevin has the advantages of training with a group, and is able to work on drafting and other techniques that Brady doesn't have the opportunity to develop as much—and so Kevin's able to get him at the end every time, because the 1,500 meters is always the last event."

The separation in points between Brady and Kevin were minuscule and it took a long time to tally them. At first, it was understood that Brady had beaten Kevin. He even called home to North Carolina and told his family that he had won a medal.

But actually, when the officials re-checked the points, it turned out that Kevin had just barely beaten Brady who ended up getting fourth place. "I don't remember the exact number now," said Brady, " but it was just a couple of points out of four thousand. That was a real great competition."

But Kevin hadn't hung around for the official scores. Disappointed over the apparent outcome, he had gathered his family and friends and headed toward Seoul's bustling shopping district.

As a result, they all missed the medal ceremony.

"When we got back from eating and shopping and goofing around downtown, there was a big case with a medal lying on my bed in the Paralympic Village," Kevin recalled. "I asked my roommate, Bart Dotson, 'What's this doing on my bed?' Bart said, 'Coach Randy Fromater left it there.'"

To his credit, Kevin immediately sought out Brady and offered his condolences—and congratulations.

Incidentally, Brady didn't leave Seoul empty-handed: he won a bronze medal in the shot put.

Finally, Brady and Kevin celebrated their renewed rivalry and friendship by staying a few extra days in Korea after the Games were over.

When Kevin finally returned to Corpus Christi, he once again was featured in a number of newspaper and television profiles, all celebrating his bronze medal in Korea.

The only dark spot on the otherwise carefree round of parties and interviews came on November 6, 1988, when another fire triggered several minor explosions in the re-built Corpus Christi Public Elevator complex. This time, however, safety features built into the structure following the disastrous 1981 explosions prevented any injuries. Still, word of the explosion had a sobering effect on Kevin. On more than one occasion, he drove by the still-smoking silos, recalling every second of the horrific day seven years earlier.

A month after Korea, in November 1988, Kevin was honored by more than three hundred friends, former classmates, and well-wishers as part of Kevin Saunders Sunday at the Downs Senior Center in Downs, Kansas.

Downs treated Kevin like a conquering hero and Mayor George Fletcher gave him the keys to the city.

"You can take Kevin out of Kansas, but you can't take the Kansas out of Kevin," Kevin told *The Downs News and Times*. "I'll always feel that the hard work ethic and honesty I was taught at home and in Kansas contributed to my success.

"They had a party for me in Downs and a big benefit

where everybody came, along with a lot of my friends from high school and a lot of friends I'd been in college with," Kevin said. "Some of my old coaches even came back for the benefit. It was really special."

The citizens of Downs were not alone in feeling pride over Kevin's achievement. Randy Snow was among those who followed the reports of Kevin's victory in Seoul with keen interest.

"It made me feel good when I'd be flipping through one of the sports magazines or newspapers and I'd see 'Kevin Saunders, #1 pentathlete on the U.S. team,'" Randy said. "Every time I saw that it made me feel good because I was there when he got started—along with many, many other people who were involved in getting him going. But just to be a little part, to be a little building block, makes you feel pretty good."

Chapter 8

Just before Kevin left for Seoul, he auditioned in Dallas for the new movie directed by Oliver Stone, *Born on the Fourth of July*. The movie was based on the book by Ron Kovic, a war vet who was paralyzed in Viet Nam, returned to the United States to become an anti-war protester, and eventually addressed the Democratic Party National Convention in 1976.

"I just happened to be in a wheelchair track and field meet in Dallas and a casting director came up to me and asked me if I wanted to take a screen test to be in a movie with Tom Cruise," Kevin said.

"I said 'Sure,' and he said, 'Come with me.' So I went with him and we went into this room where they had a video camera set up. Then they said, 'I want you to look in this camera and tell us your name and anything else you want to.'"

Since first hearing about *Born on the Fourth of July*, Kevin had been day-dreaming about making an action movie with an actual paraplegic as the star—not as a passive observer, as in the old "Ironsides" TV series—but as a genuine action-hero.

"So I looked square in the camera and said, 'My name's Kevin Saunders and I think you ought to have a *real* wheelchair guy starring in an action-packed adventure movie.' Then I proceeded to tell them what I thought.

"I said, 'Picture this: you're chasing the bad guy and he cuts across this busy street. But just before you get to the street, you notice out of the corner of your eye there's a big eighteen wheeler barreling down the road. You don't have time to stop, you're in hot pursuit, so you swerve your chair to the side and duck down low and maneuver your wheelchair between the front and back tires of the semi-trailer! You almost get the top of your head ripped off, but you appear on the other side unharmed!

"Then you hop the curb and sidewalk and resume your chase. But, while you're moving along at a high rate of speed, you look down and notice ten steps directly in front of you. You don't have time to stop or go around, so you pop a wheelie and hop down.

"Now you're catching up with the bad guy and, with the front end of your wheelchair, you knock his feet out from underneath him as he's running. As he tumbles to the ground, you whirl around in a 360 and roll right over the top of him—then burn a little rubber on his neck to teach him some manners. Then you pin his head and neck between the back tire and front tire of your wheelchair, take out the handcuffs, clamp 'em on, and then take him in and book him!"

The casting director was somewhat taken aback by Kevin's impassioned synopsis, but Kevin wasn't finished yet.

"I saved the best for last; this is the most important part," he said, while the camera continued to run. "Don't forget, don't you ever, ever forget—especially in the movies—that only *then* do you get to kiss the pretty girl."

Kevin leaned back in his chair with a contented look on his face.

The casting director smiled and told Kevin when and where the call backs would take place.

A couple of days later, Kevin got a call informing him that Oliver Stone wanted to meet him. So he went and landed a part in the movie. They began filming in Dallas, in December 1988.

"I didn't get to kiss that pretty girl (Tom Cruise took care of that, but next time... Like I say, 'there's always a way!), but he did designate me as a 'principal actor', an actor with a speaking part. That was a real honor because from then on they really treated me like royalty. I got to eat the nice meals and be around Tom Cruise and all these actors you see in movies and on television—along with Oliver Stone. It also meant I got to go inside the reserved, roped-off area during filming."

Kevin's scenes featured Kovic (Cruise) and a group of disabled Viet Nam War veterans trying to crash into the Republican National Convention, where President Richard Nixon had just been nominated for a second term.

"The filming was exciting," Kevin said. "We did some big riot scenes and it was dangerous. We were just flying by the camera, being pushed around, and punched by dozens of cops and about 500 people. There were lights everywhere, fake tear gas in the air and everybody was running at breakneck speed.

"It was supposed to be summer in Miami instead of winter in Dallas, so you had to suck on ice cubes to keep fog from coming out of your mouth when you yelled."

Shooting sometimes lasted to 5 a.m., usually in below freezing weather. Since Kevin had several lines during the climatic riot scene, he frequently found himself next to Cruise.

"When I first met Tom Cruise, he was looking at me and I was looking at him and I never did talk to him," Kevin said. "We were not far apart. I wasn't gonna say anything. I didn't wanna bother him because all these people would come up to him even on the set and between takes and want to shake his hand and say, 'Hey.' So I just sat there. I didn't want to push. I looked at him and he looked at me and that was it.

"Finally, he came up to me and said, 'Are you the guy that won the bronze medal in Seoul?' I said 'Yeah.' And Tom Cruise said, 'I wanna shake your hand, that's awesome! Can I have your autograph?'

"I said, 'Sure! Can I have yours? But I need a few for some friends.' He said 'How many you need?' And I said, 'About 500 for some girls back in Corpus Christi.'

"He just laughed. 'Well, maybe we'll get you a couple and you can Xerox 'em.'

"After that, I visited with him from time to time. He said he put a picture of me up in his dressing room for motivation. He just joked around most of the time; he's a real nice guy. He always looks straight in your eyes; he never breaks eye contact with you. He was a real disciplined person, and very intense.

"Then one night between takes, he said that he'd always felt that he never could do well enough when he was in high school. He said, 'That's why when I got into acting, I gave it everything I had—because I didn't want to let it pass me by again. You've got to make the most of every opportunity. I could have done a lot better in high school than I did. And now that chance is gone.'"

When the Dallas-area filming was completed, both Oliver Stone and Tom Cruise told Kevin how much they'd enjoyed working with him and complimented him on his work.

Kevin said the wheels of his van barely touched the ground all of the way back to Corpus Christi.

Oliver Stone also made a strong impression on Kevin.

"He's a great man," Kevin said. "He really treated me with respect and he gave me the impression that he thought I could do well. He paid big tribute to me as far as what I'd accomplished in sports. And he gave me an opportunity. He didn't have to give me that much time and attention, but he must've felt something from me from the audition interview I did."

Some of the other wheelchair parts were played by professional actors out of Los Angeles, who told Kevin that he was very lucky that Oliver Stone had singled him out to be a principal actor, thus allowing him into the "inner circle"—a privilege rarely extended to extras or even featured extras.

When *Born on the Fourth of July* premiered in Hollywood in December of 1989, Kevin was invited to attend. He arrived early, toured the town with his friend from Corpus, Dr. Tom Diaz, and stopped by Oliver Stone's office at his request. In the office, Oliver's personal secretary took him aside.

"She said, 'Kevin, don't get your feelings hurt if it isn't what you thought it was going to be as far as your part goes in the movie.' So she prepared me for the fact that they might have cut some of my footage out of the final version of the film. I never thought they would have cut my speaking lines."

In the final cut, Kevin only appears fleetingly in several scenes outside the Republican Convention. His longest sequence, following Kovic as they storm the hall, is just a few seconds long.

"They ended up cutting all my speaking lines, but Oliver's secretary told me it had nothing to do with how I delivered my lines," Kevin said. "She said it was just the sequence of the movie, and not to worry about it.

"I finally told myself that even though they cut a lot of my footage out of the movie, at least I got paid principal actor pay, and I got to be right in the middle of things. And Oliver Stone and Tom Cruise today know who I am."

As for his trip to Hollywood, it wasn't like he had pictured it. He thought it was going to be limos and photographers and glamour, but it was not that big of a deal. The screening was held in a nice theater at Universal Studios, with plush seats, each equipped with headphones.

When Kevin knew that he was going to be in Los Angeles, he contacted Ada Jankolwitz, host of the daily exercise program "Bodies in Motion." Kevin had once written her a fan letter and Ada had responded. The two had corresponded for several years. When the premiere of *Born on the Fourth of July* was confirmed, the two made plans to meet in Beverly Hills.

"She was more beautiful in person than on TV," Kevin said. "We went for a ride around Hollywood and got to take a jet helicopter ride over L.A. We flew eight feet off the surf over the ocean, then we flew over Beverly Hills High School—Ada's high school.

"Then we went to lunch and I gave her an unusual Christmas present—a music box I had found in a gift shop in Corpus Christi. I'd never seen one like it before and since Ada had been such an inspiration to me, I wanted to give her a memorable gift."

When Kevin gave it to her, she jumped up and gave him a hug and a kiss. But Ada leaned into him a little too much and tipped him over backwards! In the process, his feet got tangled under the table and *it* tipped over too—sending their meals and drinks flying!

"I lay on the floor, looked up at her and said, 'Now *that's* a kiss!'"

Ada and Kevin have continued to correspond since their memorable first—and only—date.

Born on the Fourth of July opened to strong reviews and quickly became one of the favorites for several Academy Awards. Its biggest competition came from *Driving Miss Daisy* and, ironically enough, another film where the protagonist spent much of the movie in a wheelchair— *My Left Foot.*

When the Oscars were awarded in March of 1989, Tom Cruise's wheelchair-bound American veteran lost the Best Actor award to Daniel Day Lewis' wheelchair-bound Irish writer/artist. *Born on the Fourth of July* lost the Best Picture Oscar to *Driving Miss Daisy.* However, the Academy did name Oliver Stone as Best Director.

Oliver Stone stayed in occasional contact with Kevin, even after he began making first *The Doors,* and later, *JFK.*

"He's even called me up on the phone here at my house, just to talk to me," Kevin said. "It is a great honor to get called up and be told, 'Oliver Stone's on the phone— he wants to talk to you.'"

Buoyed in part by news accounts of his work on the film, and in part by the bronze medal from Seoul, Kevin's calendar began to fill up with speaking engagements, both in schools and businesses.

Kevin also began to delve deeper and deeper into the works and seminars of motivational speaker Anthony Robbins. Anthony champions what he calls "neurolinguistic programming" (the use of language to control the mind) and is the author of *Unlimited Power.* In time, Kevin and Anthony began to correspond and eventually became friends.

It was at one of Anthony Robbins' seminars in Hawaii that Kevin met someone who would be both friend and advisor for years to come, Dan Brock. It was a two-week certification program, twelve to sixteen hours a day in "neuro associative conditioning." Kevin and Dan were on the same team of twenty people. The two became fast friends.

"Kevin and I instantly hit it off, we knew right off the bat we would be partners within the group, and that we would hang together all through the certification program until Kevin had to leave for the 1990 World Championships in Assen, the Netherlands."

Kevin's success at Seoul had already made him something of a celebrity among the 2,000 people attending the seminar. When he had to leave, Tony Robbins asked him to say a few words to the attendees.

"Kevin made a great speech and everybody said goodbye to him and we knew he would do really well because he was so charged," Dan recalled. "And I knew we'd be in touch again."

Chapter 9

In the days that followed, Kevin maintained a hectic, if sometimes erratic workout and competition schedule. In January, 1989, he finished fifth in the wheelchair division of the Houston Tenneco Marathon. In April, he won the Capitol 10,000 in Austin. He also entered smaller races in Dallas and Tulsa. In between, the City of Corpus Christi officially named April 7 as Kevin Saunders Day.

In June 1989, he traveled to Philadelphia to compete in the NWAA National Track and Field championships where he won the 200 meters, 400 meters, 800 meters, 1,500 meters, as well as the pentathlon and javelin. He also took home a silver in the discus and a bronze in the shot put. It was the best Kevin had done in a national meet thus far.

"One night during the meet I went out with a couple of friends. I told them, 'I'm going to show you just how mental competing is. I'm going to stay up all night long and I'm going to whip Jimmy Green tomorrow morning in the 400 meters.' Jimmy's a great athlete. They didn't believe me, but I did it. You've just got to want it and do what it takes mentally and physically to get the job done.

"Later, Jimmy heard what happened and said, 'Well, come to Atlanta next month and I'll whip you in the Peachtree.' I said all right, so I came to Atlanta a few weeks later and I whupped him again! The fellowship we've always shared has always been important to me. Jimmy, by the way, built my first racing wheelchair."

About the same time, Kevin noticed that his performance in the weight-lifting events was not improving at the same rate as his other events.

So in the summer of 1989, he began an extensive weightlifting program, in addition to his road work. He worked with Paul Barbie, an instructor at the Corpus Christi Athletic Club. He would work out heavy three days, then light three days, then rest on Sunday. He pumped up at an impressive rate.

"Kevin is hard to hold back," Barbie told *The Corpus Christi Caller-Times*. "He'll go out of town on a Saturday, run a marathon Sunday, and get back into town Monday morning at 10. Then he will incline bench press 225 pounds."

In addition to racing in the Peachtree, Kevin finished first in the Kaiser Roll in Minneapolis-St. Paul, held in July of 1989, and second in the Marine Corps Marathon held in Washington D.C. in November of 1989.

Other races followed, including The Woodlands Marathon (first place) and the Houston Tenneco Marathon (fifth place)—both in January 1990.

The next major meet was the Qualifying Trials for Assen, the Netherlands, held in Atlanta, March 29-April 1, 1990. Kevin again dominated the field, scoring for the first-time ever, over 6,000 points in the pentathlon.

On May 24, 1990, Kevin drove to San Marcos, Texas, to hand out awards at the Texas Special Olympics competition, and run an exhibition 800-meter race. Despite having sore arms from a full day of weightlifting the day before, he finished the exhibition with a time of 2:10. But it was the awards ceremony afterward that stuck with him.

"I learned that beauty and ability are always there in a person, the key is just to look for it," Kevin said. "Some of those competitors were the happiest people I had ever seen.

"And I learned it's very important to give to others. The real happiness comes from giving to others. I really believe it will come back to you ten-fold when you freely give to others out of the goodness of your heart."

Others were noticing changes in Kevin, including his Southwest Wheelchair Coach Judy Einbinder, once one of his harshest critics.

"I certainly think that Kevin became a real positive addition to our team because his attitude was so positive,"

Einbinder said. "Sometimes people are not in a mood to train or they're cranky and Kevin will snap them out of it with one of his canned speeches about making it to the top. But he's been very, very effective when we've had new people come out to the track."

Qualifying for the World Championships in Assen, The Netherlands, and actually competing there are two different things. Paralympic athletes have to pay their own way. A letter dated June 5, 1990, from the National Wheelchair Athletic Association was typically brief:

"You have been selected to attend the World Championships in Holland, in July 1990.

"The fee for the trip, $1,560.00, was due June 1, 1990. At this point, our records indicate that you have paid $175.00. This leaves an outstanding balance of $1,385.00."

The balance was due June 12—by then less than a week later.

Kevin and his friends immediately put the word out and donations came from a host of sources in Corpus. It was a process that had been repeated—and would be repeated again—time and time again. For equally talented disabled athletes without Kevin's support system, overseas competitions are rarely accessible.

By contrast, The United States Olympic Committee sent 591 summer athletes to Barcelona in 1992 at a cost of about $10,000 to outfit, transport, and house *per athlete.* Of those 591, incidentally, 178 finished "out of contention"—USOC doublespeak for athletes in the lower fifty percent of the field or below twenty-fifth place. Of that number, thirty-nine never even took the field.

At the World Track and Field Championships and Games for the Disabled in Assen—a small town in northeast Holland—Kevin discovered, among other things, that his systematic weightlifting regimen was beginning to pay big dividends.

"Assen was interesting because there were no divisions or classes—everyone competed for one gold medal in the pentathlon," Kevin said. He felt great that morning when he went to the practice field with Mike Collins, a coach from Houston. He threw personal records in the discus (21 meters), the shot (7 meters), and the javelin (19 meters). He also ran a personal record in the 200 meters in (31.3 seconds) and outran Jimmy Green in a training run, reaching nineteen miles per hour.

But more than that, Kevin discovered that he loved Holland. He kept thinking about how great it would be to tour Europe on a bicycle with his son Steven, maybe at age thirteen or fourteen, with the bicycle's front end hooked up with Kevin's wheelchair so that they could move at a high rate of speed.

"We could spend maybe two months touring. There are bike trails all over Holland, France, and Belgium. There are a lot of things to see and do. It is a different way of life here. I found I really need to take time to learn more."

That afternoon, a Russian pentathlete told Kevin that he wanted Kevin's "U.S.A." jacket.

"I told him he could have it if he could beat me," Kevin said, "but that if I won, what was he willing to risk? I said 'You should be willing to risk something as precious to you as this jacket is to me.'"

In broken English, the Russian said he'd ponder Kevin's question and return with a suitable stake.

"The night before the pentathlon, I taped my gloves and taped the cushion in my field chair," Kevin said. "I said my prayers and read and planned and did my mental preparation. I got down on my knees and asked God to help me do the very best I could do. I just tried to have faith and focus. I'd trained well, so I just kept my mind on what I had to do."

Kevin was one of the first people out of bed the morning of the event, found two Boy Scouts who helped him move his equipment to the track, and was one of the first athletes on the field.

"I put my American flag cap on and kept my head down," Kevin said. "I read about each event before it took place. I concentrated on each event, doing mental visualization. And after that event was over, I only thought about the next event."

He ran a good 200 meters and did just below his personal record in the shot and javelin.

While Kevin was waiting for the discus competition, he got to talking to Rudy Van den Abbeele from France. Van de Abbeele was the gold medalist in Seoul. He was again leading the competition, and the discus was his best event. So Kevin thought he had better employ some mental strategies at that point, and tried what he had been taught by Roy, a kick boxer he had met in Hawaii, who used techniques taught to him by Anthony Robbins.

"I tried to break Rudy's concentration—there's a lot of mind games you can play. I didn't *do* anything, I just asked him real innocently, 'Rudy, when was the last time you performed below your level in the discus? I mean, really, *really* below your level?' And when he was thinking about that, I tapped him on the shoulder again and said, 'Would you do that for me?'

"Rudy said, 'In your dreams, American!'

"But he was thinking of that right before he went into the circle to throw. Then I tapped him on the shoulder again and told him, 'Good luck, Rudy.' What I didn't tell him was that I'd already seen in my dreams that I had won the gold medal."

Surprisingly, or perhaps not, Rudy's first two throws went careening out of bounds and he was forced throw his third and final throw just to make a mark. The end result was a throw several meters shorter than his average.

"This was the point where I won the pentathlon, utilizing my body not just physically, but mentally as well," Kevin said. "I was about twenty-three points behind when I started the final event—the 1,500 meters. I wanted to beat Rudy by at least four seconds since you earn ten points per second.

"During the 1,500 meters, I had total focus, total concentration. I focused on what I had to do; I didn't pay much attention to the other guys. As a result, I had a good 1,500 meters and won the race easily. When they tallied the points up, I won the pentathlon by 170 points and set a new world record over athletes from seventeen countries. I couldn't believe I'd won it, but I had—thanks to God and the support of my family and teammates. God definitely answered my prayers that day.

"And, oh yeah: I was now the proud owner of a beautiful Russian military hat!"

After the meet, even Rudy congratulated Kevin on his strategy. Among world-class athletes, such "mind games" are a common weapon. Kevin just happens to be very, very good at them.

William Brady, himself a victim of Kevin's "mind games" commented that, "Kevin likes to try to psyche you out. As an athlete, you've *got* to learn to block it out. You've got to take it with grain of salt or it can mess up your concentration. Maybe that's a little edge Kevin's learned to take over the years—you gotta do what you gotta do—all's fair in love and war. And the pentathlon."

After the meet, Kevin had the title "Best All-Around Wheelchair Athlete" of the World Championships.

"That night I went with my friends John Carey and Jaap Kwast to party downtown. John spent the night at the train station so he could leave early Saturday morning on the train to Berlin. I told him I'd meet him in Paris at the Hilton or the Eiffel Tower.

Kevin's non-stop celebration continued long past dawn on Saturday and he barely made a 6:37 a.m. train to Paris.

"I had a five-hour train ride to Paris," he said, "but despite being up all night, I was wide awake. Winning in Assen and setting the new world record caused me to do some serious thinking. It kind of changed things for me.

"Before, I was always working to prove who I was, but from that point on, my reputation would be on the line every time I competed. People would now know who I was and would always expect me to perform well. It was kind of scary, especially for someone who hadn't always taken his training all that seriously in the past."

Rather than giving him the euphoric high he expected, Kevin found that setting the world record instead gave him a renewed sense of commitment—even maturity.

"Somewhere in France, I realized personal motivation

and philosophy is something you grow with all the time. It's not anything that can be set in stone. Discipline and hard work are the cornerstones of success. I don't think anyone can dispute that. Now I had to go out and do it every time in every race."

Once in Paris, Kevin and John Carey tried to cram a week's worth of sight-seeing into a single day and both fell asleep exhausted in the hotel. And, once again, Kevin overslept and almost missed the train to Amsterdam for the flight back to the U.S. at 5:00 p.m.

Once back in Corpus Christi, Kevin wrote a host of thank you letters to his sponsors and friends. One of his first letters was to Dan Brock.

Dan immediately picked up the phone and called Kevin.

"We talked for about an hour about all kinds of things," Dan said. "The second I mentioned I wasn't really happy with my situation in northern California, he said, 'When you break that off, would you mind coming out and helping me develop a marketing plan for myself?' He knew I'd had some pretty good successes already, and we liked each other's drive and motivation."

In August 1990, Kevin gave the commencement address to 270 Del Mar College graduates and another 2,000 people in the Del Mar auditorium in Corpus Christi. During the ceremonies, Kevin gave the college's president, Buddy Venters, the gold medal he'd won at the National Track and Field Championships in 1990.

The Corpus Christi Caller-Times reported part of Saunders' address in the August 27 issue:

"Life is neutral. It doesn't take care of you, it doesn't destroy you. It's there for you to do with what you can... If it is to be, it's up to me.

"Losers are the ones who don't get into the race."

Meanwhile, Dan was tying up loose ends in California. He arrived in Corpus in early September for what he thought would be a two-week stay.

Once at Kevin's house, the two men exchanged notes, proposals, and ideas about Kevin's prospects as a motivational speaker.

"It was all nice, then something happened that changed my whole life," Dan said. "I was in Kevin's office and I was looking around at all the plaques on the wall and I said, 'Where are all of the gold medals?'—because Kevin has won hundreds of gold medals.

"Kevin said to look under a certain file in his cabinet. So I looked and there were snapshots of kids with gold medals around their necks. I turned around and I looked at him and said, 'Kevin, you gave your gold medals away?'"

"Kevin said, 'Yeah. Why?' It was no big deal to him.

"But my eyes watered and I turned away from him.

"Then Kevin said, 'I would feel guilty hanging gold medals up on my wall, knowing they could make a difference in a young child's life, especially a child that went through the hell I went through—or even worse. I couldn't hang those things up on my wall. I know I'm the best in the world and that's good enough for me. Hey, you want one? I'll win one for you, too.'

"He was so easy, so confident, so giving to others, it blew me away," Dan added. "From that moment on, I didn't know how long it was going to take me—I didn't care how long was going take—but I vowed that I was going to make damn sure that as many people as possible got an opportunity to meet this guy. Especially children."

Dan returned to California after two weeks, gave up his partnership, took his clothes, put the rest of his belongings in storage, drove back to Texas, and moved into one of the vacant rooms in the back of the complex at 4209 Live Oak.

His belongings are still in storage, three years later.

Kevin and Dan have never had a written contract. But from that point on, Dan has served as Kevin's manager, agent, publicist, driver, head cheerleader, and best friend.

Dan has also become a tireless advocate of the disabled—although it's not a word he likes.

"No one is really handicapped *or* disabled," Dan said. "Those words shouldn't be used. What is walking for any way? To get from point A to point B, to go places and do things. Well, I don't know anybody who goes to more places or does more things than Kevin Saunders—and yet, because he doesn't use his legs to get there, he is labeled as disabled and as handicapped. That pisses me off! Those are labels—not people!

"Statistics are showing that employers all around the country are finding that not only is it advantageous to hire those people because of tax reasons, but also that these people are dynamic, ambitious, and driven. They love to work, they want to work, they're an inspiration for people around them and they become a real asset to the companies they go to work for. And we're calling *them* handicapped?"

Dan said that while he's helping Kevin achieve his goals, he's also helping a movement.

"Kevin will be an influence on not just the disabled, but able-bodied people as well," he said. "That makes me feel so good. Even if I didn't make any money at it, I would just feel so satisfied in what I'm doing.

"What's happening is going to affect everybody. There's a new wave of optimism moving among the people who are physically challenged and with that wave comes a whole new realm of opportunities for everybody. Everybody will win."

Dan threw himself into representing Kevin, making contacts, setting goals, raising money.

Meanwhile, life in the wheelchair athletics fast lane continued without a break for Kevin.

Kevin's first meet after joining up with Dan was the Pan American Games in Caracas, Venezuela, in September 1990.

The Pan American Games are rarely as contested as their counterparts in Europe and Asia. The United States team dominates against much weaker competition. Consequently, for many of the athletes, the Games are often closer to mini-vacations than the standard meets athletes are used to.

The only competition that Kevin had was William Brady. Of course, Brady beat Kevin in the field events— the shot put and the javelin. But when it came time for the pentathlon, Brady was chasing Kevin, as usual.

"We were real fortunate in Caracus because the USA team stayed at the Hilton. That was totally out of character for the USA team. They normally put us in military barracks or dorms with eight to ten to forty guys to a room! Here we had two people to a room and this place was plush. We were eating in a dining hall. The guys serving the food had big uniforms on with towels on their arms. Very nice."

The relaxed, luxurious surroundings created a meet that quickly became legendary in wheelchair athletics circles—and not just for the on-field exploits!

"Caracus was the most incredible free-for-all I'd ever seen in my life—*none* of those guys were innocent," said one coach. "I've traveled around the world with them a hundred times and I had never seen anything like it. I mean, some guys who were happily married would get out of the elevator with three women draped over them.

Shortly after arrival, American officials warned the team that certain parts of downtown Caracus were off-limits—for the athletes' own safety.

"Soon as they told us that, Kevin got a taxi and went into town!" William said. "Kevin's wheelchair has a pouch underneath where he keeps his money. So when the taxicab driver put Kevin's wheelchair in the trunk, he somehow found Kevin's pouch. And Kevin had about $150 in the pouch. So all of a sudden, Kevin's flat broke—only he doesn't know it yet.

"Meanwhile, there was a bar in the Hilton. Unbeknownst to us, all the girls at the bar were prostitutes. We thought the girls just liked Americans! I'm sitting there with another of the field event guys and we're talking to some beautiful Venezuelan women in real short skirts—really hot-looking girls. We'd bought them a beer and we were all drinking."

Suddenly, William noticed that Kevin was gone.

"He'd long since met up with one of these girls and he thought she was in love with him," William said. "He thought she was the hottest thing in the universe! So he disappears with her up to his room. Once there, she started saying, 'How much money?' This caught Kevin by surprise—he still didn't know she was a prostitute.

"Now remember, Kevin didn't have much money, maybe ten to twenty dollars, which, still naive, he gave her. This totally offends this woman! She screamed at him, took Kevin's money, flushed it down the toilet, and stormed out!"

Judy Einbinder is quick to point out that Kevin—indeed, many of the wheelchair athletes—is often pursued by young women wherever he competes.

"Kevin usually has a little trail that follows him around every place he goes; he does have a collection. None of the guys do too poorly, they all have a line—and it works! I've gone out with them and watched it happen and it is just amazing.

"First, I think the women are not threatened by them and whatever shred of nurturing instinct they have comes out. First they think that they're just going to take care of these guys—ha ha ha—and the guys will milk it—and take whatever they can get.

"The next thing they know, they're surrounded. I've seen it in crowded clubs: my athletes surrounded by four or five women. Maybe it is the curiosity thing, too. Whatever it is, these guys are not shy. Each one of them has a line that just won't quit. They do all right for themselves. They've left their mark around the world— and Kevin is right up there!"

Still, according to William, the rest of the stay and the return home from Caracus was miserable for Kevin.

"Everybody on the whole American team immediately began picking on him, saying things like, 'Say Kevin, can I borrow five dollars?' There are quite a few stories about Kevin—and they're all true. He's a character."

But, as Judy is quick to point out, all of the ribbing is done in affectionate fun. And woe be to the person who is not part of the wheelchair fraternity who picks on one of their members.

"Those guys are very close," she said. "There is not anywhere near the glory in field events—and the pentathlon is considered a field event—that there is in track events. They're a minority, to begin with, and they stay together. They're there for each other. They all want to win, but more than that, they all want to see the sport advanced. And they want to see their people recognized and appreciated, particularly in the pentathlon because there are many, many different skills that have to be in top form in order to excel in the pentathlon. They're a tight little fraternity."

Chapter 10

Back in the United States, things were heating up for Kevin in other arenas as well. On January 29, 1991, with twenty-four hours notice, he was invited to travel to Washington D.C. to meet first with Sen. Bob Dole, and second, with then-President George Bush. The White House is a long way from a farm outside of Downs, Kansas, but Kevin handled the meetings with his usual aplomb.

"Senator Dole is from Russell, Kansas, about fifty miles from Downs," Kevin said. "His neighbor was the engineer that built the track around my high school at Downs and I guess Bob Dole read about me in the papers. Also, a couple of ladies from Downs had written him letters about me and there was an article in his hometown paper about me giving the track to Downs High School. Senator Dole wanted me to meet the President of the United States. So after meeting with Senator Dole, I was driven over to meet with President Bush in the White House.

"I was a little nervous, I didn't know what to do or say, to tell you the truth, it all happened so quickly. Suddenly, there I was and the President came out from behind his desk and said, 'Kevin, I've heard a lot about you. You're a real inspiration and it's a real pleasure to meet you.'"

Kevin, never at a loss for words, said, "Well, it's a real honor to meet you, Mr. President. I thank you for signing the Americans With Disabilities Act. On behalf of myself and the millions of disabled Americans that you've empowered throughout the United States, I would like to present you with this gold medal I won while competing as a disabled athlete for the United States of America."

At that point, Kevin gave the president one of the gold medals he'd won at the world track and field championships. The medal was attached to a brass plaque

that read, in Kevin's usual understated manner, "To
President George Bush, I truly believe there's always a
way. God bless America. Kevin Saunders, World
Champion."

"President Bush said, 'I can't accept that, Kevin.' I said,
'It'd be a real honor for me if you'd accept it. I know
you'd do the same for me.'"

After the impromptu medal ceremony, President Bush
asked Kevin about the famed backwards wheelchair
somersault he'd perfected.

"I said 'Well, you start rolling backwards like this...'
and one of the aides ran up and said, 'No! No! Not here!'

"Then the president started looking at some pictures
Dan had brought along and suddenly said, 'You know,
you look like you're built up like Arnold Schwarzenegger.
We need to get you and Arnold together on my council
for Physical Fitness.' He turned to Sen. Dole and said,
'Let's get Kevin on there.'"

For Kevin, who had only begun to dare dream about
being appointed the first disabled person to the President's
Council on Physical Fitness, it was like a dream come
true. For once, he was speechless.

The trip back from Washington D.C. was filled with
frenzied conversation. Dan had already begun generating
some revenues by selling Kevin as public speaker. But
they promptly decided to add a systematic letter-writing
campaign in support of Kevin's possible nomination to
the President's Council on Physical Fitness to Dan's duties.

Kevin received another boost shortly after returning
from Washington. Dan's contacts with Southwestern Bell
produced a month-long speaking tour to motivate the
sales forces at the major Southwestern Bell offices. Not
only was the pay good, but it was good exposure as well.
And with the daunting odds against Kevin being chosen
for a PCPF position, every bit of media exposure helped.

"It started with a big sendoff party for the Southwestern
Bell management," Dan said, "which turned into a really
great relationship all the way around. It was a nice way to
start off a speaking career, to get a taste of what was required."

Kevin and Dan learned how to optimize Kevin's performance. For example, they got him a wireless microphone—which came in handy while Kevin was doing 360s in his wheelchair! There are a lot of little details that have to be considered when the speaker is in a wheelchair: stage platforms and ramps that have to be built to spec, different kinds of sight-lines from the audience, etc. But Kevin was a big success.

"Kevin does his own thing when he's on stage." Dan said "He might use only one word out of a speech I give him, which is OK because he does just fine on his own. He is a very, very good public speaker. Most crowds love him; they go nuts over him."

After the speaking tour, Kevin resumed his competition schedule. Among his more notable meets were the Woodlands Marathon (since he'd won it in February 1990, he was invited back in February 1991 to defend his title— all expenses paid), the March 1991 Wichita River Festival 10K (at which he not only won, but set a new course record), and the Dallas Regionals Track and Field Meet, April 26–29, 1991.

In Dallas, Kevin took home the gold in the pentathlon, javelin, discus, and shot put.

"The Dallas Regionals were a regional competition requirement for the up-and-coming Paralympics in 1992," Dan said. "Kevin was awesome, he cleaned up, no one could touch him. It was as if he was in a league of his own. He won four gold medals."

Afterwards, Kevin and Dan rushed back to Corpus Christi where Kevin had a standing appointment at the Ada Wilson Children's Hospital. Kevin had established a special relationship with the staff and children at the facility for mentally disabled and severely deformed children.

"These children identify with Kevin like they do with no other doctor, no other nurse, no other person in their family, no one in their whole life," Dan said. "Kevin is it to them—he's everything. It was apparent from the very first five minutes we were ever there in front of them.

"When we first went, the staff said the kids would probably like it a lot, but they went nuts. You can't imagine the level of noise! From the moment he rolled into a ward, there was a tidal wave of screaming. It continued the whole time he was there. After the first time, it got to be funny. There was no sense in holding it back because it was hysterical. The nurses cracked up, too. Even the kids who couldn't see him started howling.

"Kevin is used to people listening in silence when he talks because his story is so powerful. But at Ada Wilson, there was always somebody screaming or groaning or making some sort of noise. Then suddenly there was a really wild noise from the back—*Yeaarrrgghhh!* and the volume increased. When that happened, they surged forward just to touch him.

"Each time this happened, I would go out in the hall and cry, then clear my eyes and come back in. I was crying with joy, not because I was sad."

Kevin has since been a regular visitor to the hospital. Among his most loyal "fans" is a young African-American with profound mental and emotional disabilities named Rorie (not his real name).

"Rorie is really special," Dan said. "His mind is completely out there and he can't talk very much, but he understands what you're saying. And when he's happy, he howls *'Yooooooo, yahyahyahyah, whooooo, dadadadablalalalah,'* which we found means everything from 'I love you' to 'Give me that' to 'I wanna touch that.'"

Rorie's screams increased whenever Kevin came to visit. It got to the point that whenever Kevin was at the hospital speaking or just hanging out, Rorie would see him and begin his animalistic scream—and not stop.

Kevin would then turn and say, "Hey Rorie! Come over here!" and Rorie would jump up—he's super hyperactive—and run over to Kevin and Kevin would grab him affectionately by the neck and say, "I'm trying to give my speech so you go back and sit down and shut up and I'll come see you in a minute!" And Rorie would do it.

After a quick trip to Downs High School for

Commencement on May 21, where Kevin gave the graduation address, he and Dan were invited to the Texas Special Olympics Track & Field meet in Corpus Christi. Kevin had been asked to be one of the Texas Special Olympics "celebrities." He handed out medals and spoke at the banquet that night.

At the event, Kevin met with the sponsors and promoters next to the bleachers for a time before noticing that he was slowly being surrounded by a small army of electric wheelchairs driven by the children of the Ada Wilson Hospital in Corpus.

"They all knew Kevin and they are creeping up on us and saying, 'Kevin, Kevin!'" Dan said. "But the one we both noticed was a guy who was severely deformed, who could barely lift his head up and speak. Suddenly, he was standing on his feet in front of Kevin, and he managed to croak out over and over again 'U… S… A! U… S… A!' God! we all lost it! But Kevin pumped his fist for him and shouted 'All right!'"

The rest of the ceremonies were relatively uneventful until Kevin wheeled out on the track to congratulate the winners.

"Suddenly, we could see Rorie coming," Dan said, "howling and baying with joy. He was like this flash, bounding across the field with his eyes really wide, screaming, *'Aaaarrrooooo! Kevin! Aaaarrrroooo!'* We needed to finish up with the winners, so I said, 'Kevin, give him your mobile phone, let him call someone!'

"So just as Rorie arrived, Kevin said, 'Rorie! C'mere! Do you have a girlfriend?' And Rorie threw back his head and howled *'Whooooo!'* So Kevin said, 'Do you wanna call her?' That really pleased Rorie, so he screamed *'Yarrrrr!'* He took Kevin's mobile phone and *pow!* he was gone! Rorie takes off sprinting with the phone and you can see him moaning into the phone, doing laps around the track, as happy as can be.

"Kevin had an entourage the rest of the day. It's so magical to see those kids. He does more with those kids than the doctors can do."

At the Special Olympics banquet dinner that night, Kevin was given the Civic Leader of the Year award— much to his complete surprise—over a host of better-known Texans.

Dan had contracted with a full video crew to capture the ceremonies and Kevin's talk, as part of his promotional media package. But until you've been to a Special Olympics banquet with fifteen hundred participants, you can't imagine the scenes of complete and total joyful chaos.

"It's just noise, that's all it is," Dan said. "A thousand little people grunting and screaming and standing and running—not just the Special Olympics athletes, but the brothers and sisters and parents who'd have to jump up every so often and chase down a child. There were only a few people who could have even heard Kevin's talk that night."

Dan and Kevin learned a lot from the event, though. They sharpened their presentational skills. They realized that you can't have the same presentation for children as you do for salesmen.

The video of the evening wasn't usable as a marketing tool, but Dan and Kevin still put it into the video recorder from time to time, if only to hear the undulating wail of Rorie cutting through the crowd noise, a delighted, primeval *"Aaaarrrroooo!"* that wobbles and warbles in the background.

With Dan's help, Kevin continued to gain in regional name recognition. In July 1991, Dan met with Sharon Wallace and Tom Curlee, executives from Central Power and Light Co., and signed a six-month contract engaging Kevin to speak at schools across Texas. Part of the deal included two television commercials for CP&L starring Kevin, which were widely shown throughout South Texas.

The CP&L tour was another great learning experience and extremely gratifying as the company was not only interested in doing something for the community, but wanted to help Kevin achieve his goals. They provided Kevin and Dan with extra money to put together a beautiful brochure and a marketing videotape. The response was tremendous from the schools and the kids. It was so well received that CP&L signed up again for 1992 and into 1993.

Becky North, CP&L's education programs advisor, said that the power company was delighted with Kevin's work, both as a motivator and a symbol of perseverance.

"Education and the success of students in our service territory and throughout Texas is a top priority at Central Power and Light Co.," Becky said. "CP&L's sponsorship of Kevin Saunders's tours is another strong link in the company's continuing commitment to education."

Becky drove Kevin in the CP&L van to virtually all of the schools in the forty-four-thousand-square-mile district. Since he was in training for Barcelona, she also ended up being his unofficial trainer as well, running with him on the track and spotting for him in the weight rooms!

On July 10–16, 1991, Kevin competed in the Victory Games in Long Island, New York. This was a national meet and he won gold medals in the pentathlon and javelin, a silver in the discus, and a bronze medal in the shot put. Vice-President Dan Quayle attended the event.

In fact, New York itself seemed so much fun that Kevin and Dan decided to stay over an additional six days, partly because they would have had to return to New York in that time to fly to the Stoke Mandeville Wheelchair Games in England later that month.

The two saw all of the standard tourist spots—the Statue of Liberty, the Twin Towers, Rockefeller Center—and ate at a host of ethnic restaurants.

Finally, Kevin admitted to Dan that he'd always wanted to ride the subway.

"I said, 'Kevin, it's not wheelchair friendly. These are steps from Hell. It's not worth it.'

"Kevin looked at me and said, 'I'm a champion, I can do it!'

"So I said, 'If you really want to do it, we'll do it. But be prepared because I'll have to be carrying you up and down a *lot* of steps.'"

And that's what he did. He put Kevin on his shoulders,

carried him up eighty steps, placed him on a step, then went back down the stairs, got his wheelchair, and carried *it* to the next platform—where there were *another* eighty steps!

"So that's how it was, and I really didn't mind it. If he wants to experience it, I'm all for it. But I did want him to know it was not the most wheelchair-friendly place."

Finally, Dan and Kevin ended up in Grand Central Station and made plans to ride the subway to Rockefeller Center. At Grand Central, they became friends with two buskers, or subway musicians. The two offered to help Dan carry Kevin and his wheelchair up several long flight of stairs, where they took the same train. The musicians got off at 42nd Street to catch yet another train.

As the foursome waited for different trains, Kevin asked the two musicians to play a song.

They both looked at each other and said, "For you, we will." So they opened up their cases and they jumped right into a song. Kevin put his sunglasses on and started dancing in the middle of the waiting platform.

All of a sudden—*whoosh!*—a train pulled up. The doors opened and Kevin asks, "Is this my train?" Dan had all his camera equipment out, taking pictures, and said "Yeah, but..." When he turned around, Kevin was in the train and suddenly—*whoosh!*—the doors close and the train took off.

"The look on Kevin's face was, 'Whoops! I think I've just blown it big-time!' Then the train disappeared, heading for Harlem. Kevin knew nothing about the subway. He had no money, no identification. All he had were his sunglasses."

After several minutes of sheer panic, Dan decided to catch the next train for Rockefeller Center, where he kept an anxious vigil. The only time he left his post by the subway station was when he went to the bathroom—and even then he left a note with the subway guard and asked her to watch for a young man in a wheelchair.

"I said, 'Watch for this wheelchair guy because he doesn't know New York. He doesn't have any identification or money and he's lost, so keep an eye out for him because I have *got* to go to the restroom.' She just kept looking at me suspiciously and saying, 'A guy in a *wheelchair?'*

"I dashed all the way up and then dashed all the way back. When I got back, she pointed to Kevin and said, 'He's here.' Kevin rolled up and said, 'Hey. What's happening?'"

Once Kevin had realized he was on the wrong train, he had gotten off at the next stop and followed the directions to the platform that would take him back the way he came. Once there, he removed one of his velcro straps, strapped the wheelchair to his leg, and laboriously crawled up eighty steps to the next platform, one step at a time. He repeated this maneuver several times—and was nearly trampled a number of times by crowds of people rushing off one train or hurrying to meet another—until he arrived at Rockefeller Center. During that long process, not one New Yorker offered to help him with his wheelchair.

"Kevin always says, 'You gotta go for it!' Lost in the subway with no money? 'No problem,' he says, 'There's always a way.' He really believes that. If there's one thing I've learned from Kevin, it's that there truly *is* always a way."

But Kevin and Dan's excellent adventure in the Big Apple wasn't over yet. The day before they were scheduled to leave for London, Kevin decided to take advantage of a rare New York heat wave and visit one of the beaches. So, despite Dan's pleas to the contrary, the two found themselves deposited just outside of Montauk Point and Long Beach on Long Island. But neither man was prepared for the sight of what appeared to be a million New Yorkers packed cheek to jowl on the sand.

Kevin shouted, "Holy Toledo! This is insane!" There was no wheelchair access at all—but that didn't stop Kevin. Dan told him he couldn't go into the sand on his wheelchair because it would take two hours just to reach the shore. Kevin said, "I don't care. I'll do whatever it takes to get there."

Kevin, who doesn't like to be helped in front of people unless it's absolutely imperative, took two full hours to get to the water.

"The only reason he wanted to go was to find some babe, some girl. But New York is not like Texas. You don't just walk up to somebody and say, 'How's it going? Isn't it a great day today?' because they'll look at you and snarl, 'Get outta here!' And that's exactly the response he was getting after he had struggled for two hours to only go about two to three hundred yards in very soft sand to where the crunch of people were."

Finally, even Kevin's perpetual high spirits were shot down and he decided to return to the parking lot. After about an hour, Kevin said, "Dan, you're gonna have to help me here. I'm getting so fatigued I can feel my muscles tearing." Since the important meet at Stoke Mandeville was only a couple of days away, Dan agreed—stifling the urge to say "I told you so."

"Instead, I told Kevin, 'You carry the camera bag and I'll pull you,'" Dan said. "I strapped a couple of straps to me and I started pulling. We didn't care what people thought, although it looked pretty pathetic. Along the way New Yorkers kept saying, 'What's *he* doing on the beach?' I wanted to drop everything and grab them and say, 'The same thing you're doing here. You got a problem with that?!' but I didn't like the odds. Like a million to one.

"Finally one guy yells, 'Hey! You want some help?' I said, 'Hallelujah! Sure!' And once we had two guys, we turbocharged Kevin from the beach onto the pavement in no time."

The victories on Long Island qualified Kevin for the 1991 World Wheelchair Games in Stoke Mandeville, England, from July 17–26.

The flight to Stoke Mandeville was uneventful, until about halfway across the Atlantic Ocean. Kevin turned to Dan and, in a hushed voice, asked "Are you ready?"

"Then he says, 'You're gonna have to hold up the towel,'" Dan said. "I said, 'For what?' He said, 'I'm going to have drain my bladder [via a catheter].

"There's always a way."

LIVE YOUR DREAMS
Kevin V. Saunders
WORLD CHAMPION

Kevin V. Saunders
World Champion

in a promotional shot for Central Power & Light Company.
t: Robert Maxham

(top right) Kevin on the Cloud County Community College soccer team, 1974.
Credit: Downs News

(upper inset) Kevin, two years old, at the family farm in Downs, Kansas.
Credit: Saunders Collection

(middle) Kevin [back row, second from left] and Jack Myers [back row, fourth from left], team photo of the Kansas State University Rugby Club, 1977 state tournament champs.
Credit: Saunders Collection

(lower) Kevin [#10] as a running back for Pratt Junior College.
Credit: Saunders Collection

Blood, bodies were scattered all over

/E ANTON
ICE MILLAR

lood and the suffering
omprehensible.
.ed and torn bodies
d unattended on concrete
t. A few cried. Others
onscious.
moke billowed from sev-
.n silos as the first fire
rrived at the scene.
the gates of the Corpus
'ublic Elevator, bodies
cattered everywhere.
ooked as if all the injured
n accounted for, more
ere found under massive

ic, confused workmen
mong their fellow em-
ot knowing whom to help
ingle ambulance had ar-
d the two attendants ran
body to the next.
.an grabbed an ambu-
end nt by the arm and
o an injured friend. Then
mother injured man and
er attendant in that direc-

ing lot next to the silos
ke a battlefield. Small
blood formed beneath
the injured while teams
men scurried to find
ft splints and stretchers.
ed blown-out doors and
ions and scraps of lum-
arry the victims to the
ce and several private

lood was splattered on
and in several areas,
the spots where men
ed or fell helpless to the
The injured lay on top of
s of concrete, metal and
lation that littered the

ressure from the ex-
rew me three or four
e air," recalled employ-
Reyna, 19 "I turned my

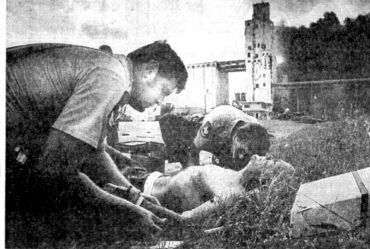

Paramedics Stanley Harper (L), Rex Callaway assist unidentified injured man as grain elevator burns
(Photo by Lee Dodds)

back and ran. I couldn't see nothing There was just a lot of smoke
in front of me. I could see just a
little bit."
Reyna, who was standing inside
a warehouse loading dock at the
time of the explosion, sat on a

grassy slope and watched the
growing flames as he spoke.
Others less fortunate than Reyna ran from the scene, their skin
smoldering and emitting the pungent, sickening odor of burned
flesh One man, his clothes

burned away and his face swollen
from the burns, brushed by a reporter and cried to him for help
The man's left eyeball was pro-
truding from its socket and a portion of his left ear had been
burned away. His flesh began to

ripple and buckle.
"I saw a guy running down the
road towards me who had severe
burns and all he had on was a
shirt collar with a few threads attached. His hair was singed."
See Suffering, page 12A

medics assisting an unidentified man as the grain elevator burns.
it: Lee Dodds, *Corpus Christi Caller Times*

1e scene of the explosion, Don Bray, the man at the far left later carried
n from the wreckage on a door when the rescue teams ran out of stretchers.
it: Lee Dodds

The concrete grain silos, over a hundred feet tall
and one and a half feet thick, with reinforced
steel, blew apart like paper.
Credit: Lee Dodds

Kevin during a weekend visit,
seven months after the explosion.
Credit: Robert Hays

Lawyer Joe Jamail [left] and his
friend Kimball Simpson.
Credit: Saunders Collection

Kevin's lawyers who took over h
case [from left to right], Doug Al
Guy Allison, Steve Hastings, and
Albert Huerta. *Credit:* Dan Brock

Kevin with Robert Hays, 1983.
Credit: Saunders Collection

Saunders to be on the big screen

December, a movie the best film yet for ...ons Cruise and Oscar-... director Oliver Stone is ...ed to premier.

...the best part for local ...goers is that joining ...on the silver screen will ...n Saunders, formerly of ...

...e movie, "Born on the ...of July," Cruise plays ... of a Vietnam soldier ... wounded and returns to ...ied States a paraplegic, ... to spend the remainder ...fe in a wheelchair. ...ders, who became a para-...in real life after being ...300 feet in a grain eleva-...losion in Corpus Christi, ...lays the part of one of the ...pped individuals Cruise ...friends with.

..."s it like to be on a real ...et with Cruise and Stone? ... a real neat experience," ...anders excitedly.

...gh he didn't have a ...le, Saunders said Stone ... to take a liking to him ... used him to a principal ... a result, Saunders "got ...real special."

...got to be inside the ..., roped-off area during ...and had a dressing room ... name on the door.

...ing for Saunders took ...ound three months ago ...ed about a week and a ...We put in a lot of hours," ...nders. "It wasn't all fun. ...as a lot of hard work, but ... also a lot of hurry up ...i."

...e night scenes, Saunders ...ooting sometimes lasted ...a.m. And it was cold — ...ly below freezing.

...the scenes were sup-...o be taking place dur-...summer in Miami rather ... they had to suck on ice

cubes so their breath wouldn't form steam.

For the movie, the Dallas Con-

country.

During the protest, Cruise gets thrown down the steps of the

vention Center was transformed into the Miami Convention Cen-ter where Cruise and his friends had gone to protest the treatment Vietnam veterans were receiving after suffering debilitating war injuries in the defense of their

jersey with the number 83 which belonged to Jack Myers of Downs, Saunders talked to and

convention center. Cruise didn't use a stunt man but wore football pads for protection. Saunders said the scene must have been shot about 20 times.

Dressed in an orange and black Oklahoma State football

real that two individuals actually received broken legs.

One of the policemen in the

was beside Cruise during the en-suing riot scene. Remembering, he laughed and said, "Some girls would have killed for my posi-tion."

The riot scene itself was shot about 10 times. It became so

One souvenir is an auto-graphed picture of Cruise. The other is a personal letter from Stone.

In the letter, Stone thanked Saunders for his "enthusiasm and performance" in the movie.

While Saunders enjoyed his movie-making experience, his ultimate goal is still to change the image people have toward the handicapped.

"This small part that I had in this major motion picture will hopefully give me the positive exposure to go on to bigger and better things," Saunders said.

With the movie and other ex-posure paraplegics and quadra-plegics are beginning to receive, Saunders and others like him feel the time is ripe to let people know they are capable of many, exciting things.

Saunders said he loves to go to movies of the "Rambo" variety. While watching them, he envisions the scenes being performed by a "wheelchair Rambo."

This has prompted him to collaborate on a forthcoming novel with a paraplegic as the successful, exciting leading character.

A short prologue will tell the story of Saunders' life; how he grew up in Downs, participated in athletics, went to college, was injured in the explosion, went through rehabilitation and worked to go to Seoul where he won a bronze medal in the 1988 Paralympics.

Through the movie, the book, inspirational talks, his own life and his accomplishments, Saun-ders hopes to show that life doesn't end when someone is suddenly confined to a wheelchair. It can mean a new even more ex-citing life is just beginning.

That's especially true if Saun-ders' motto is applied: "Go for it 110 percent."

ON FILM SET—Jim Stuart and Kevin Saunders, number 83, ham it up for the cameras while on the set at the filming of "Born on the 4th of July." Both former Downs residents. Saunders had a principal part in the film and Stuart was an extra. riot scene was another Downs resident, Jim Stuart.

Though picture-taking of the actual filming was not allowed, Saunders did come away with some prized keepsakes of his experience.

...n with Jim Stuart, both of Downs, Kansas, on the set of *Born on the 4th of July.*
...it: Osborne County Farmer

Article featuring Kevin training for his second Peachtree Road Race in Atlanta, notice old hospital chair in the background of photo Credit: Lee Dodds, *Corpus Christi Caller-Times*

[left] Article featuring Kevin on the track he donated to his alma mater, Downs High School, 1985. *Credit:* Diane Gasper-O'brien, *Hays Daily News*
[right]Article featuring Kevin at the Olympic games in Seoul.
Credit: Ely Marsh, *Corpus Christi Caller-Times*

World Championships and Games for the Disabled Assen 1990

Kevin being interviewed back in the U.S. after the World Championships. *Credit:* George Gongora

Kevin competing at the World Championships. *Credit:* Stephen McCarty 1990.

Kevin's father, Donald Saunders at the Olympic stadium, in Seoul, 1988, wearing the broze medal that Kevin won there. *Credit:* Duane Saunders

1, the day he broke the world record in
·entathlon making him the "best all-around
lchair athlete in the world."
t: Stephen McCarty

Kevin presents his World Championship gold medal to President George Bush in appreciation of the President's role in promoting physical fitness and for his support of the Americans with Disabilities Act.
Credit: Official White House Photograph

In the waiting room next to the Oval office prior to their meeting with President Bush are [left to right] Kansas Congressman Pat Roberts, Dan Brock, Leah Buikstra, Kansas Senator Robert Dole, Mike Hand, and Kevin
Credit: Fredrick O. McClure

d Schwarzenegger presents Kevin with
)istinguished Service Award.
*: Dan Brock

Chairman Arnold
Schwarzenegger
proudly presents Kevin
as a new member of
the President's Council
on Physical Fitness
& Sports.
Credit: Dan Brock

with [left to right] Franco Columbo, Joe Wieder,
Fischer, and Leah Buikstra.
*: Dan Brock

Kevin pushing the shot put.
Credit: George Gongora

Kevin throwi
the javelin.
Credit: Georg
Gongora

Driven to Win

Imagine running backward as fast as you can, slamming on the breaks, throwing your head back and completing a full flip only to land upright. Sound like a tough stunt? Kevin Saunders can do it ... and in a wheelchair.

"You've got to get going real fast backward and then slap the wheels to stop them and then just go like you're going to dive back in a pool," explained Saunders, a 1978 graduate of Kansas State in agricultural economics. "You've got to make sure you have that chin tucked tight or you're in for a rude awakening."

Saunders will do virtually anything he sets his mind to. He is driven. But everything he does is a struggle.

In 1981, he was thrown 300 feet onto a concrete parking lot in the worst grain elevator explosion in south Texas history. Ten others were killed in the blast that broke Saunders back and left him with no movement in his body below his chest. He was in the hospital for a year. No one, including himself, expected him to survive.

Today, Saunders is training to compete in the wheelchair pentathlon in the 1992 Barcelona Paralympics for which he is the favorite. He won the gold medal in the 1990 World Championships and earned the title of Best All-Around Wheelchair Athlete.

He now makes a living as a motivational speaker, speaking to high schoolers and children in hospitals about the only thing he knows: "What it takes to deal with change and adversity in your life, how you do that, how I did it."

Conditions that might breed despair in most people add fire to Saunders' optimism. He has turned the credo 'there's always a way' into a way of life.

He trains more than six hours each day. A 60-mile track workout is an average day, not to mention pumping weights and exercise bands at other times.

"It's not bad for a man who, out of a chair, cannot sit up.

"Sometimes it seems that the odds are too tough, that you just want to quit because it's too difficult. But if you just hang in there ... you'll reach your goals," Saunders said.

As proof, Saunders competed in his first road race in an old hospital chair. It was hardly a winning effort, but he refused to quit. Now his accomplishments serve as motivation to anyone — able and disabled.

"You have to encourage them to focus on the positive and try to take life and be optimistic and say that you can have what you want if you believe in it," he explained.

The drive of Saunders, however, started before the accident. As an undergraduate at K-State, he competed in track, football and was a part of the 1976 rugby team which won the Big Eight championships. He also graduated with Phi Beta Kappa honors and had a started promising career as a federal grain elevator inspector.

Somehow, Saunders has turned his tragedy into something positive.

"I constantly remind myself that my accident occurred for a purpose — a purpose that will provide me with even greater opportunities to make a positive difference in the lives of others," he said.

"If you knew you couldn't fail, what would you want to do?" he asks.

As if to answer, Saunders has been working, with the help of Senator Bob Dole, to become the first person with a disability to be appointed to the President's Council on Physical Fitness.

In fact, in a gesture symbolic of his entire life since the accident, he presented his World Championship gold medal to President Bush as a gift.

Between now and the Olympic trials in Salt Lake City on July 13, Saunders can be found throughout the country at various competitions for wheelchair athletes. Or he will be at his Corpus Christi home doing what he always does — living by his word: "Work hard and don't lose faith. It's all I know to do."

Kevin Saunders hurls a discus from a new chair designed by K-State students, including onlooker Brad Eisenbarth.

K-State engineering students developed a revolutionary new chair for pentathlete Kevin Saunders

(Left to right) Daniel Brock, assistant to Saunders, and Brad Norman, Brad Eisenbarth, Drakash Krishnaswami aid the athlete.

Wheelchair athlete Kevin Saunders always thought the equipment available to him was inadequate. While racing wheelchairs had made great technological strides, chairs for field events hadn't evolved much past the hospital wheelchair. That bothered him.

In the middle of April, Saunders contacted his alma mater with a challenge: design and build a better wheelchair for athletes with disabilities.

The challenge turned into a mechanical engineering class project at Kansas State University. The students with the best design would then build it and Saunders would in turn use it in the Olympics.

By early June, students in the class had designed and engineered two chairs — one for the javelin and discus and another for the shot put.

The winning ideas were from Brad Eisenbarth, Paul Snider, Maury Wilmoth, and Brad Norman, all of whom sacrificed several nights' sleep to engineer and assemble the chairs. Two professors, Drakash Krishnaswami and Daniel Swenson, advised and aided in the work.

What the new chair does is spin like a swivel-chair so an athlete can create circular momentum for the discus and javelin. In a normal wheelchair, a person cannot create forward momentum.

Both chairs were designed specifically for Saunders' needs, and while not perfect, they may lead to further advances in the needs of wheelchair athletes.

"This is a prototype. We hope that it will lead to more interest and research," explained Krishnaswami.

Saunders said the idea of the spinning chair was not his own, but that he was the first to make a move toward having one made. "Nowhere in the world do I know of a chair that spins yet," he said. "People with disabilities are going to be taking part in a lot more activities of life and doing it in a way that's as close to being on your feet as possible. That's why the wheelchair that spins is something unique to be able to do the field events.

"We're still getting the bugs out of it right now, but it is going to add a little excitement and interest to the sport," Saunders said.

But will it add distance to your discus?

"Definitely so," he said.

Due to it's unconventional design, the spinning chair may be found to be illegal for the Paralympics. Saunders explained, "Whatever happens, at least we made the effort. It will go eventually, I know that. It's good to be right there at the beginning and to know that we initiated it."

The other chair is modeled on chairs already in use for the shot put. It is mounted on a more stable base and angled further forward than other field chairs to give Saunders more leverage on the toss.

Despite the long hours of hard work to build the chairs, the students found the project to be interesting and self-motivating.

"It's a good sign to show that things are really changing for the better for all people," Saunders said. "It says a lot for the university to be willing to do something like that."

Shortly before he departed with the new chairs for a competition in Oklahoma, Saunders told everyone who worked on the project, "You guys will have part of that gold medal from Barcelona."

Text by Jay Seaton

Photos by Rod Mikinski

---

in the Manhattan Mercury featuring the development of new field chair s for Kevin by the Kansas State Engineering Department's students and staff. Brad Eisenworth and Rod Mikinski, *The Manhattan Mercury*

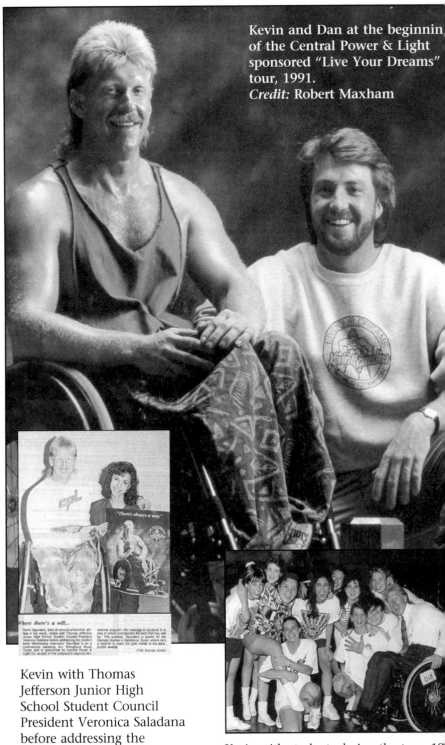

Kevin and Dan at the beginning of the Central Power & Light sponsored "Live Your Dreams" tour, 1991.
Credit: Robert Maxham

Kevin with Thomas Jefferson Junior High School Student Council President Veronica Saladana before addressing the student body as part of the tour, 1992.
Credit: Tish Dumas

Kevin with students during the tour, 19
Credit: George Gongora

Kevin during a hospital visit, encouraging and inspiring children that "there's always a way." *Credit:* George Gongora

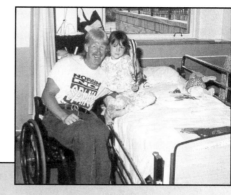

Kevin as a volunteer at the Special Olympics.
Credit: George Gongora (above)
Credit: Mike Collins (left)

Kevin at his home
Corpus Christi wi
[from left to righ
Dan Brock, Suzie
Cantu, Kent Olive
and [below]
Kevin's son Steven
Credit: George
Gongora

Kevin in the New York City
subway, July 1992.
Credit: Dan Brock

Kevin in his racing chair with his favorite good-luck charm "Woodstock."
Credit: George Gongora

Kevin with Elizabeth and Senator Bob Dole and Dan
Brock at the 1992 Republican National Convention.
Credit: Saunders Collection

Kevin on the "Live Your Dreams" tour, 1992, during the filming
of a commercial for Central Power & Light.
Credit: Dan Brock

Kevin holding the bronze medal he
won for the pentathlon, with Kent
Oliver [left] and Dan Brock.
Credit: Saunders Collection

"'But Kevin, there's somebody sitting right next to me and someone across the aisle!' And for the first time, Kevin looked at me with pity in his eyes. He said, 'What do you think I'm gonna do, Dan? Hobble to the restroom in the back? I don't have my chair, and even if I did, it's too wide for these narrow aisles. Besides, the bathrooms are too narrow for me. This is how it's done.'

"I'd never thought about it before. So that's what we did."

Dan strung a towel up so they wouldn't have to worry about the aisle. Then he tucked a towel from Kevin's shoulder to the tray. If someone came by, he would just take a towel and cover himself. It was strictly standard operating procedure for Kevin since they don't have gurneys on planes and they have no way of getting physically challenged people to the restroom facilities. They have to do it right there.

"That is really sad because there's no reason he should be humiliated like that. Only a few planes have small wheelchairs. Physically challenged people should be able to fly and be comfortable, too."

Once in England, Kevin did well, winning a silver medal in the pentathlon. As an experiment, meet officials allowed a quadriplegic to compete in the paraplegic pentathlon and, with the complicated weighted points system, the quadriplegic handily won the medal. Kevin still retained his title as the best all-around athlete in the paraplegic division.

Once the Games were over, Kevin decided it was time to celebrate. Among those who were celebrating with him was William Brady, who believes that a certain amount of celebrating is healthy for parathletes.

"One of the sacrifices athletes make is that we're always in training, always watching our diet," William said. "We always have to avoid all the good times our friends are having, especially during the summers when everybody is out partying, going to the beach. When the competitions are over, we're the first ones to blow off steam. The important thing to remember is that it *is* over, that this is *not* a chronic lifestyle. It's a way of rewarding yourself for all of the hard work you do."

After the competition in Stoke Mandeville, there was a big dance for the athletes. Brady went to the parking lot to get ready to go back to the barracks where he and Kevin shared a room. Suddenly, he saw Kevin sitting alone in the dark and said, "What the hell are you doing, Kevin?" And Kevin replied that he was waiting on a taxi to go into the town.

"Well, Stoke Mandeville didn't really have a town. It was a rural, country village at best. But he had met some babe and he was going to catch a taxi and go into town.

"That's our Kevin: the first thing he wants to do when we finish a competition—find him a woman and have a party!"

Coincidentally, Kevin's brother Duane was in London during the Wheelchair Games in Stoke Mandeville and the two made plans to get together during the week.

"But Kevin never showed up," Duane recalled with a laugh. "He's great about saying things like, 'Hey, I'll meet you there.'

"I called him when we got home and asked him where he was. He came up with some story about not being there on those days. I don't know whether to believe that or not. Something—or, more likely, someone—probably came along that was more interesting than me!"

The next major hurdle before the 1992 Olympics in Barcelona were the U.S. Paralympic Trials in Salt Lake City, which would be held in June, 1993. In the meantime, there was much to occupy Kevin's time.

With Dan's help, Kevin signed with a major commercial talent agency in Los Angeles, in hopes of landing parts in print advertisements, commercials, television shows, or even motion pictures. Dan spent six months researching various agencies and agents before settling on one.

While the agency worked hard on Kevin's behalf, nothing substantive came out of the agreement.

It was also during this time that Kevin settled his final lawsuit. Diane Sanders of the firm of Henkel, Hyden & Sanders in Corpus Christi was forced to file for Chapter 7 protection to protect Kevin's remaining assets and annuity on April 19, 1991.

"Kevin found himself early on, after he got his personal injury settlement, dogged by people wanting to sell him on various investment deals—and anything else," Diane said. "It was, at that point in time, one of the few things that made him feel good about himself—helping people with his money. Along the way, he made several pretty bad investments. And once he got into those bad investments, he couldn't raise cash flow for the real estate notes. It wasn't long before his monthly payments exceeded his cash flow.

"Kevin struggled with this for several years until it got to a point in the late 1980s, through various defaults and foreclosures, that the lenders who had lent him money to get into deals wanted their money back. And Kevin was forced to take money out of his personal injury settlement. He could only do that for so long before his income wasn't sufficient to cover either the debts, or his living and medical expenses."

Once Kevin began to miss payments, Diane said, the various lenders started foreclosing on him and took back his collateral.

These foreclosures occurred at a time when the value of real estate in Texas was at an all-time low. Consequently, when the creditors foreclosed, they got relatively little in return for their investment. But Kevin had begun buying real estate as an investment when real estate values in Texas were high—the early 1980s.

So in the late 1980s, when he was trying to sell, real estate values were at their lowest. When lenders took the property back, Kevin lost both the investment and his assets and he *still* owed them money! The same lenders couldn't get back their money out of the collateral or assets, so they wanted it from somewhere.

"It was tough deal for Kevin," Diane said. "He got sold on these deals back when he had some cash to put down on them. He'd use his personal funds to kick a venture off, then have to borrow additional funds to pay the monthly notes when the hoped-for cash flow wasn't happening.

"When all of his lost assets were purchased, he still owed lenders a lot of money. But it wasn't just Kevin, the same thing happened all over Texas. A lot of people invested heavily in what turned out to be bad real estate investment deals."

Ultimately, certain lenders tried to take judgments—or get what was owed them—satisfied out of Kevin's monthly income from his annuity, which was his only source of regular income. It was at that point that Kevin went to Diane and they made the decision to file for Chapter 7 protection and to claim, as his exemption, his annuity.

"There was a risk attached since it wasn't entirely clear under the law whether we'd be able to keep the entire annuity," Diane said. "So it was sort of a gamble, although I was relatively confident he could keep at least some of it."

"So we filed Chapter 7 and claimed the annuity as his exemption. But one of the largest creditors objected, so the case went before bankruptcy Judge Richard Schmidt in Corpus Christi."

Judge Schmidt heard the evidence and listened to the legal arguments. He then called both parties back a couple of days later.

The judge ruled that the annuity was exempt. The judge acknowledged that, aside from paying his medical expenses, the annuity funds needed to be maintained so that Kevin could earn a living through his speaking engagements—and that the funds were an essential part of his health and well-being.

Of course, everything else was lost: the real estate, all of his investments, all of the funds he put into them, everything. But he kept his annuity, his house, his personal vehicles, his household furniture, clothes, and personal belongings.

The Judge Schmidt's decision was unusual in that he decided to deliver his decision orally, rather than written and later read.

"It was probably the most memorable judgment I've ever heard," Diane said. "The judge was very impressed with what he'd heard. Once he heard Kevin's story with all of the details, the nature of the injury, and the extent he'd been paralyzed, how he'd overcome everything and was earning his living through motivational speeches, he had no choice but to rule for us. It was very emotional for all of us, it was an inspirational speech by the judge, and it was a memorable few minutes for me."

"I'd been in the court system since the grain elevator blew up and I never got out until then," Kevin recalled. "They took me all the way to bankruptcy and then they figured they couldn't get any more out of this guy, so now they're going to leave me alone I guess. All the settlement money's gone except what I get each month. And that's the end of that."

Though the bankruptcy hearings took more than a year to complete, Kevin had no choice but to continue to train and compete. At times, he found himself again slipping dangerously close to despair. He tried at those times to "party" his way out of depression.

"Sometimes I took the 'playing hard' stuff a little too seriously," Kevin said. "My journal entry for one day in early 1992 shows that for dinner I had four Orgasms (a drink served in a *large* shot glass), three lite beers, two margaritas, and one Kahula and coffee to go with my club sandwich and fries! Needless to say, I did not feel too good the next morning. Looking back over my journal, I realized I was hitting it pretty heavy there for a while."

For a while, Kevin's moods swung wildly. Early in 1992, he entered a period where he lost his taste for the non-stop training regimen.

"I don't think he was enjoying training, I think he was getting burned out at last," Jack Myers recalled. "Of course, any professional athlete is going have trouble keeping himself in focus all the time.

"I went to see Kevin at a track meet in Norman, Oklahoma, at the University of Oklahoma. Kevin was in bad shape—not physically, but mentally. He was complaining about everything: the track wasn't right, his chair wasn't right, he needed to put different wheels on it, any excuse to make himself feel better. Kevin was doing horribly.

"So, in the middle of the meet, Dan Brock and I said, 'What are we going to do? If he's in this kind of shape, and this kind of mental attitude, he's not going to make it." So they left the meet, went downtown, bought a calendar, and marked July 19, the day the U.S. trials in Salt Lake City would begin. They decided that Kevin had a training problem and knew they had to get this schedule into his head. So for the rest of the afternoon, they sat up in the stands, watched him, and figured out the schedule.

After the meet was over—which Kevin won anyway— the three friends went back to their hotel and talked.

Dan then told Kevin, "If you don't start training better, if your attitude doesn't get better, you might as well kiss everything you've worked for goodbye."

The next step, they decided, was that Kevin needed to start training with better racers in Houston, because racing was his weakest event. He agreed to move to Houston in June or July of 1992.

"That day he did a 4:50 in the 1,500. I started calling him every other day, urging him on. We all began working on him and eventually we brought him out of it—he was in a burn-out stage, but came through. Everybody has ups and downs, that was his down. But he rebounded fast."

Kevin's next important meet came with the regional games in Austin. He'd regained his will to win, but, for the first time, he was unsettled by his new-found position of *having* to win the gold in Barcelona.

"Especially now that I was working with a talent agency in California, and because of all of the work Sen. Dole was doing with me on the President's Council on Physical Fitness, and because of my own financial problems," Kevin said. "I had all of these people counting on me and here I was self-destructing because of fear. I thought I could overcome it, but my focus was not there. I knew I had to be smarter in the future.

"Still, I managed to do OK in Austin. My races were not as good as I needed them to be, but I did show some improvement over a couple of previous meets. My times were 18.6 seconds in the 100 meters, 34.4 seconds in the 200 meters, 2:15 in the 800 meters, and 4:11 in the 1,500 meters. I threw the shot 6.17 meters, the discus 18.92 meters, and the javelin 17.50 meters when I got a good sticking throw.

"One thing that did come out of that meet was that I noticed some of the other athletes' field chairs seemed to be stronger, more stable than mine. I didn't want to get beaten in Barcelona because someone had better equipment, so I sat down and began to think what I could do about it.

"I found my answer in Manhattan, Kansas."

Chapter 11

Kevin had kept close ties with his alma mater since leaving Kansas State in 1978. He'd frequently been a visitor whenever he was in Kansas to see his parents in Downs. And he'd become acquainted with the head football coach at Kansas State, Bill Snyder, a two-time Big 8 Coach of the Year and ESPN National Coach of the Year. Kevin had also become friends with Bill's daughter Meredith, age seventeen, who had survived a devastating automobile accident in high school which left her with only limited use of her arms and hands.

"The first time I visited her in the rehab hospital she seemed in real good spirits," Kevin said. "I told her to focus on the positive, what she *could* do. I took her a little lion from *The Wizard of Oz* with a badge of courage on it. I told her that it was a symbol of the courage inside each and every one of us that we can pull out whenever we need to overcome obstacles in life. I said, 'Meredith, don't give up because there's always a way. Just to play hard and work harder.'"

In the Spring of 1992, Kevin made contact with various offices at Kansas State. He'd already been featured on the cover of the school's alumni magazine and knew a number of the faculty and administrative staff.

When his initial contacts proved promising, Kevin and Dan flew to Manhattan, Kansas, where they met Jack Myers. Kevin's plan was to visit various administrators and department chairmen personally to plead his case.

Among the first to meet Kevin was Scott Scroggins, who had only a few months earlier returned to K-State to work as an assistant to the dean in the college of engineering. Scott recognized Kevin from his photos, took the three men to the Mechanical Engineering Hall, and introduced them to the Dean of Mechanical Engineering.

"They were looking for some funding, and they did get some from the President's office and the College," Scott said. "Kevin and I stayed in touch through the spring and when he returned to K-State in June, it was to begin work with the crew of two professors and four students on his wheelchair design.

"I really feel the decision to help Kevin came from all the interested parties: the professors and students, the engineering department, and the university itself. I realize you can't take up the special interest of every alumni, but Kevin is special in more than one way. It's not just that he's physically challenged, it is his ambition, his energy, and the good will created through his many activities, as well as the lives he touches, and the hope that he brings others.

"It really was a super project, a chance to work on something with a real-life impact. And with the ADA, it certainly had a lot of current events interest. It just seemed right for the school to help somebody with a profile of past accomplishments and future goals like Kevin Saunders."

The two professors who were most intrigued by Kevin's problem and who subsequently took the lead in the study were Dr. Prakash Krishnaswami and Dr. Daniel Swenson.

In April 1992, there was an announcement from the Provost office of the university that Kevin had approached the University asking for assistance and gave a number to call if anyone was interested in helping out. Prakash was teaching the Engineering Graphics #2 and thought that working with Kevin on a wheelchair design would be a good project for the course. The more he and Dr. Swenson thought about it, the more interested they got until they decided to actually do something, and that's when they called the Provost office and the dean of engineering.

Prakash Krishnaswami, an associate professor of mechanical engineering, accepted the administration's invitation to work with Kevin and the two began several months of telephone conversations while Kevin continued to train in Texas.

"But even though most of our initial contact was over the phone, we got to work on plans and designs," Prakash said. "We actually started building the prototype at the end of the semester and the first few days of June.

"What appealed to us about a wheelchair re-design was that it was an intriguing concept from an engineering point of view. It was a very interesting, non-trivial problem where so many factors needed to be accounted for and where there had been so little done. Dr. Swenson and I were also interested from a standpoint of both helping Kevin, who we were really impressed with, as well as all wheelchair athletes in general. We thought this problem offered substantial benefits to others in wheelchairs."

The two professors were not surprised to find that there were a host of problems that had to be addressed before a true re-design could even begin.

"One was that the existing designs didn't brace him enough," Prakash said. "Another was that Kevin got most of his power from pulling on the vertical post by the field events chair. That just didn't seem to work too well to us. Plus, the Paralympians were all using the same chair for different events. Our study led us to believe that you need different positions, different chairs, for different events—which wasn't possible with the existing design of the field chair. Kevin thought they needed a device that would allow the chair to swivel, for instance. But existing chairs were not very stable, so one of the early things we tried to do was minimize the movement of the chair itself.

"The other problem is that no two disabled people are alike. They may be paralyzed in totally different groups of muscles. The chair that we worked on specially for Kevin, I'm not sure yet that we could generalize for the population at large."

The researcher's pilot study identified a pretty extensive—and expensive—design problem. Given enough time and money, the engineering department could make a lot of progress—and still not be close to solving the basic problem of creating a better chair for paraplegic athletes. And time, particularly with the U.S. Wheelchair

Athletic qualifying meet in Salt Lake City approaching so quickly, was not something either Kevin or the university had in abundance.

"About that time, Kevin came up for several days to work with us," Prakash said. "We'd done some of the preliminary design, including one crude test model we needed to make measurements of Kevin's body from. During those three or four days, we probably spent several hours each day together working on the project."

Unfortunately, the design team had less than a week. They did ,however, manage to build two chairs: one that swiveled and one that didn't—for the shot put. The first chair was designed for all three field events.

"On June 2, Kevin took the spinning field chair outside Durland Hall and gave it a test drive in a drizzly rain," Prakash said. "The shot put throw felt OK, except he felt that the handle was too far out and the seat was too flat and hard—which made his balance worse. Afterward, he and the design team talked about it and decided to start with a completely new design for a backup. They hashed around a few ideas and came up with a pretty good design.

"We tried to design it in such a way that while the seat would swivel, there was still a braking system," Prakash said. "We also tried to design a moveable post that all the athletes could use. We really did not have the time to do design iteration. Usually, in a product such as this, you just can't get it right the first time. In a design that's as complex as this one, you design it and build it, but when you actually test it is when you see where certain things need to be fixed. We saw then that the braking mechanism on the swivel chair needed to be fixed, for instance, but we didn't have time to do it. We'd like to have had more time on both wheelchairs and, hopefully, there will be some time in the future.

"Still, it was a lot of fun, but hectic. For the last four or five days there it was non-stop with the students, staying up every night to 2:00–3:00 a.m.

"Kevin should come up periodically to work with the engineering department because he's such a good motivator. While he was here, despite being so deeply involved in his Paralympic training program, he still came out day and night. He'd handle all of the media attention and still come out to the workshop to evaluate our designs, make suggestions, and—sometimes—just keep us going."

As the week ground to a close, what the harried team designed was a totally re-built field chair. Unlike the racing wheelchair, the parathlete's field chair has no wheels. Wheelchair athletics rules currently limit the field chair in the height of the seat. Additional rules prohibit any kind of mechanical devices, including steel springs or any objects that can propel the athlete. Field chairs are traditionally tied down with stakes, much like a camper will stake down a tent. Each wheelchair athlete has a customized field chair.

The newly designed field chair looked quite different. It was engineered to give Kevin more balance in the chair itself. A balance point is important because without it, someone with Kevin's level of disability, a chest-level paraplegic, will lose their balance easily. Kevin has a lot of power and strength, but as he explodes forward through a movement, he loses control of his body. When that happens, Kevin loses all the advantage of that strength.

"What we're looking for is a balance point, a way to keep the power throughout the whole movement, with the force on the object," Prakash said. "Without that balance, for example, a paraplegic athlete's performance in the shot put is hindered in much the same way a quarterback, who is throwing a football as he falls off-balance, is not going to be able to deliver the ball as well as he could have if he'd remained on his feet, and retained his power through the entire movement. So that's what we're looking for as we try to change the field chair.

"It could be something as simple as how you strap your legs, it could be the way you make the seat itself and what type of support is around it, it could be the way the back brace is constructed, where you put the stop piece—all of these things can have an impact. There are a lot of variables involved and you've got to take time on each particular variable. You can't change a whole bunch of individual variables at once, because if you do, you're not going to know which one affects or improves or takes away from your performance. You've got to do one thing at a time and that takes time."

The Manhattan Mercury devoted an entire page to Kevin and the team in an article titled, "K-State engineering students developed a revolutionary new chair for pentathlete Kevin Saunders."

Jay Seaton reported that the team of professors and students had developed and engineered two prototype chairs, one for the shot and discus, the other for the javelin. The shot and discus chair spins like a swivel seat in a bar, Seaton wrote, enabling athletes to create a circular momentum.

Kevin told Seaton that the idea for a spinning chair was not his own:

"But nowhere in the world do I know of a chair that spins yet. People with disabilities are going to be taking part in a lot more activities of life and doing it in a way that's as close to being on your feet as possible.

"We're still getting the bugs out of it right now, but it is going to add a little excitement and interest to the sport."

The new field chair also has more a modern look. Made out of aluminum and steel and painted black, it looks more like a piece of state-of-the-art workout equipment than a wheelchair.

The re-designed javelin chair was comparable to existing stationary field event chairs, but was mounted on a more stable base and angled further forward than current chairs—both improvements were designed to give the athlete more leverage.

Excited by what she was seeing in the mechanical engineering lab, Kansas State's new director of public relations, Cheryll May, put together a media package on the story and worked the Wichita and Kansas City markets. Cheryll arranged a demonstration/press conference that was well attended by area TV stations, all of whom shot extensive footage.

Unfortunately, the spinning chair just wasn't ready. They worked on it some more, changing things, making adjustments, but eventually they realized they couldn't make it perfect in a day—or even a week.

Still, Kevin told Seaton and the other reporters that he feared the chairs, even if finished on time, would be ruled illegal for Paralympics.

"Whatever happens, at least we made the effort," he said. "It will go eventually, I know that. It's good to be right there at the beginning and to know that we initiated it."

Kevin and Dan submitted the new chair designs to the rules division of the international governing body of athletics for wheelchair athletes—the ISMGF. As Kevin had feared, the ruling body decided in record time that the revolutionary chairs would not be eligible for use in Barcelona in 1992.

"But that's something that may come about in the future," Kevin said. "We didn't want to risk it at this point in time because I didn't want to get to Barcelona after training in this chair and have them find a way to disqualify me."

Prakash took a scheduled year-long sabbatical following his work on the field chairs, but retains an interest in the project.

"There are definite improvements that can be made. But that's true of everything. We haven't solved the transportation problem after two-thousand years and we still don't have the perfect chair. Like most problems, this one is open-ended. It is something that would need to be worked on for years and years."

Kevin, for his part, had nothing but praise for the support Kansas State had given him.

"From the beginning, the school has taken an active role in making state-of-the-art technology available for the betterment of people of disabilities," he said. "It is an incredible opportunity to work with such innovative engineers. I think the work they're doing there will someday become known around the world, not just to disabled people, but to all athletes. They've got the power to open up whole new avenues of opportunity for the disabled to succeed—and inspire people from all walks of life. It's kind of neat being in on the beginning of something important. It took a lot of foresight on their part."

Upon his return to Texas, Kevin met with engineers like Tony Hernandez from Custom Controls Co. in Houston to continue modifying the K-State prototypes right up until it was time to leave for Salt Lake City.

Kevin has also started working with a company called Top End out of Tampa, Florida, with Chris Peterson and George Murray. Peterson does all of the welding and the actual construction of the chairs. He took a design by wheelchair athlete Jim Knaub and modified it. Jim was a world-class pole vaulter before he was injured in an accident, and now he's a world-class wheelchair racer. He designed this chair as one solid piece of tubing that's about three inches around with a couple of pieces coming down just to support that one bar.

"You stick your legs and whole lower body in something like a big pocket," said Kevin. "This makes you more aerodynamic and more stable as well. The front wheels are sixteen to twenty inches and the back wheels are the regular twenty-six-inch wheels."

Chapter 12

The summer of 1992 was particularly tense as Kevin continued to feel the pressure of heightened expectations. To compensate, he began training even harder for the Paralympic Trials in Salt Lake City.

"This meet was real important," Dan said, "because if he messed up somewhere—like the games preceding the World Series or the Superbowl—one loss and you're out. If Kevin messed up somehow, he wasn't going to Barcelona."

Kevin moved from Corpus to Houston on June 20, 1992, because there was a higher level of competition among athletes in Houston. He was training with John Rendon, Juan Rios, and John 'Andy' Anderson. They were all fast racers. The first day out he was right behind Andy—who is one of the fastest parathletes in the world—for about five miles before tiring. A couple of days later he was road racing with John and after about four miles he hit a crack in the road on a turn and lost both tires! That was a jolt! He went back home, glued them back on, but it wasn't long before they both came off again. He called it a day after that.

Kevin trained some under the coach for Southwest Wheelchair Athletic Association, Judy Einbinder, then the head coach of the National Wheelchair Athletic Association, who was based in Houston. But mostly, Kevin trained with or alongside Paul Barbie, Rocky Rodriguez, Jan Matthern, Rick Gore, Randy Snow, Jeff Sewell—as well as Andy, John and Juan.

Kevin's apartment in Houston was courtesy of Jack Ryan, a Corpus Christi businessman who became a friend through the First United Methodist Church in Corpus. Jack obtained use of the apartment from yet another friend, Fred Rizk and his wife Sylvia. The Rizk's apartment was in a perfect location for Kevin, with easy access to the gym, to the University of Houston track—and even the famed Galleria Mall!

Kevin had daily track practice at the University of Houston. After that, it was on to the Gold's Gym on Richmond Street, where Ken Beisel, the manager, had given Kevin a free pass to workout there, in preparation for Barcelona. Ronnie Tovar, a trainer at the gym, helped to push Kevin and keep him focused.

"We saw Coach Einbinder once every two or three weeks, but the rest of the time I'd train with John, Andy, and Juan. There's a lot more intensity when you're co-training that you don't have alone—like going out and doing seventeen miles wide open!

"So from that standpoint, moving to Houston helped me a great deal. I needed to work more on the track and road work to attain all of my goals. I had to do what I needed to do to win the gold medal in Barcelona. It took a lot of hard, hard training."

The training was the most intensive, exhausting Kevin had ever known. All three—John, Andy, and Juan—were strictly track athletes and trained exclusively in the speed and endurance events. Kevin, of course, had to train in the field events and do his weightlifting as well. Later, all three converted to pentathletes.

The intensity of the training sessions meant that there was little time for chit-chat among the athletes. Still, Kevin and John Rendon managed to hit it off.

John taught Kevin some techniques: like how to re-tape his gloves, or how to buy rubber boots, or how to use some of the padding John used. Kevin also found out how to use sandpaper on his rubber tires so that when he pushed, the grip was a little rougher, and how to get his elbows up high and push through the push rims. He discovered that he had been using a push rim that was a little bit too big and wasn't allowing him a full stroke down through the push rim itself.

The other main benefit about training in the Houston

summer heat was that it allowed Kevin to train with his ten-year-old son, Steven. The custody agreement allowed Steven to stay with his father for one month each summer. Steven was now old enough to regularly aid and participate in the workouts.

Steven started helping his dad in his workouts at the track when he was around eight. He would help fix breakfast and pack the drinks when they would go to the track. When he was nine, he started by putting Kevin's chair in the back of the truck. Now at ten, he helped him train by going and getting the shot put, javelin, and discus after Kevin threw them. He helped him move the heavy field chair (weighing over one-hundred pounds) to the field, hammered things into the ground, and timed Kevin when he raced. He even videotaped Kevin training.

"We hit it hard every day," Kevin said. "Sometimes we wouldn't eat our first meal of the day until two in the afternoon. Sometimes Steven would say, 'Dad, I'm hurting a little.' Maybe he'd sprain an ankle or bump a knee or cut a finger. I'd say, 'If you want to be a champion, you've gotta go when you're hurting. You've just got to tough it out, suck it up, and go for it. That's how you become a champion.'

"Sometimes he'd say, 'But dad, I don't know if I want to be a champion.'

I'd say, 'I know you do. You can't fool me because I've seen you work hard and you never give up.'

"Or sometimes he'd say, 'I want to go play video games' or 'I want to go to a movie.' And I'd say, 'Son, anybody at your school can do those things. But how many people are going to get a chance to shake Arnold Schwarzenegger's hand? How many can help their dad get an Olympic medal? We can't give up now; we can't quit. This is what it takes to be a champion. No matter how bad it hurts. This is what I've got to do this summer. That medal will be yours someday—think how proud you'll be.'"

Kevin's persuasive monologues eventually won the day.

"In the end, it feels really good to see that my dad's in the Olympics," Steven said. "It's easy to talk to other kids about my dad because almost everyone in my school knows who he is. I have pictures of him hanging up in my room and they'll ask me whole bunches of questions about him. Everybody in my school that knows about him likes him.

"And he always takes time out for me. One day we may be doing a lot of stuff, the next day he'll take a half of a day off, to go see a movie or play video games."

Fortunately, being out on the UH track until dark every day had other unexpected benefits for Steven—and Kevin. They had the opportunity to meet Carl Lewis and the other Olympians who trained there. Steven also got to see Carl's two Ferraris one red, one black.

"I was real proud of Steven, he did a great job," Kevin said. "For a kid who was just ten years old, he really showed a lot of character, maturity, and responsibility.

Kevin called his son his full-time trainer. They listened to motivational tapes and read motivational books together, they worked out together, and went to the wheelchair designer together. "I treated him like a little brother. I'd say 'Steven, how can we figure this out? What can we do?' We were always thinking, always planning, always drawing, always trying to figure things out."

At last, the Wheelchair Athletics-USA National Championships—better known as the Paralympic Trials— arrived. From July 14–19 in Salt Lake City, Utah, hundreds of athletes converged. Among them were eight pentathletes.

A day or two prior to the competition on July 14th, Kevin went to get a massage from a massage therapist about 7:30 p.m. She put a couple of hot pads on Kevin— and forgot about them! He got burns the size of tennis balls near his tail bone. Kevin hadn't even felt them, didn't even know he was burned until the next morning, when he got up to get ready to leave for Salt Lake City and noticed a wet spot on the back of his wheelchair. Kevin looked in the mirror and was shocked, worried both at the seriousness of the injury and of the possibility that he wouldn't be allowed to compete. It was a broken blister and the heat had apparently burned through a couple layers of skin. Kevin had to use healing cream and cover it with big bandages. "It scared me. A lot,"Kevin said.

"My son Steven was there the whole time, and until I left for Salt Lake City, he was the one who got up each time and changed the dressing on my burn. He put the coffee on each morning. He slept right by my bed every night, especially when I wasn't feeling well. He had his own bedroom in the Houston apartment, but he wanted to sleep next to me. I couldn't have done it without him.

"In the end, he hated to leave when his mother came to get him. He cried. So did I."

Kevin arrived in Salt Lake City feeling bad and worried about his burn.

To make matters worse, he had fallen asleep on the plane with his head on the lap tray and got a kink in his neck that was killing him. He couldn't even turn his head sideways. Kevin, who normally reveled in the challenge of overcoming setbacks, was worried because of the stiff competition he was facing on the field. "I was afraid because there were some really great athletes competing and only two slots open for Barcelona.

Once at the hotel, Dr. Ann Marie Glenn looked at Kevin's burn and said it wasn't as bad as it looked. She suggested another healing-type salve and it seemed to help.

Then, to top it all off, Kevin found out that night, that instead of Friday or Saturday, the pentathlon was to begin the next morning, Thursday, at 8:00 a.m.!

Finally, he just decided he had to relax and do what he knew he could do something about. He asked the massage therapist who was with the team to do his neck before he went to sleep. Then he asked the doctor at the high school to treat his burn again, and the doctors told Kevin he would be able to compete Thursday. Kevin went to bed as early as he possibly could Wednesday night and tried to put everything out of his mind and until he finally went to sleep.

Kevin rose early Thursday morning, still weak from the burn and still stiff from the crick in his neck. He immediately began focusing his concentration on the events rather than on his discomfort. At last, the pentathlon began.

"The four guys I was really worried about were William Brady, John Rendon, John Anderson, and Larry Hughes," Kevin said.

"The shot put went OK. I was right in there, close to what I usually throw—about 6.32 meters. I was right in the middle of the standings with my best throw—the shot put tends to be my worst event anyhow. There were no great throws from anybody that day—but at Barcelona I knew there would be, from guys who can throw a lot further than me."

Kevin won the javelin with a throw of 18.12 meters. John Anderson suffered through several below-par throws and was virtually eliminated early. John Rendon had probably the second-best throw. And Larry Hughes, who supposedly had phenomenal potential, fouled out. He attempted three throws and didn't stick one of them. "You have to make a mark to get points," said Kevin.

"The rule of thumb I always go by is to make sure the first one is a mark. Then you can let her go with the second two. But if you go all out on the first two and don't break the ground to make the mark, then you're looking at the third javelin and you've *got* to mark—and you're not going to get the distance you would otherwise."

The 200 meters provided one of the exciting moments of the competition. Kevin finished second, only 00.14 of a second behind John Rendon—a 31.74 to John's 31.60.

"By now, I had gotten the idea that if I could do the next two events OK, I could break the world record," Kevin said. "All I had to do was throw a good discus and my goal was to run a 3:50, 1,500 meters."

But near-disaster struck in the discus. Kevin, still daydreaming about a world record, let his concentration lapse. His throw of 18.68 meters was well off his personal best.

"It was not a good throw for me," Kevin said. "I knew it, too. I knew if I had thrown the discus twenty meters I would have had a shot at the record. But the heat was beginning to wear on me, being outside all day long. I was a little down. It was afternoon by then. Still, it was OK. Only Brady and Larry beat me, so I actually finished second overall after that event.

"I don't like to compare myself with other people. I don't know where others are at because I just try to focus on myself. Otherwise it takes away from what *I'm* trying to do. Any multi-event coach will tell you that. You can't really watch the other guys. You have to focus on what you've got to do—and no one else."

When the distances were posted, Kevin had a feeling that he still had an outside chance at the world record. It all depended, as always, on a stellar performance in the 1,500 meters.

"In the 1,500, everybody goes at once," Kevin said. "I was in lane one, the lane I like. That way I don't have to worry about being out on the end and having to try and get around everybody. I like to get out in front in the beginning, then I just try to run the race.

"I believed I could run in 3:50, which would have given me the record. I told myself, 'You need a 3:50, you *got* a 3:50!' over and over again. I learned this technique from Mary Lou Retton in the Olympics.

"Then I thought, 'You want to relax a little bit, actually. You feel good and you're just going to hammer it from the get-go and take off. You're going to get her going, get out of there. You're not going to get caught up in all the people.'"

Kevin's original plan was to reach seventeen to eighteen miles per hour for the first lap and stay at above fifteen miles per hour for the remaining three laps.

But more important than monitoring speed was the actual time it took to complete the 1,500. In the pentathlon's complicated scoring system, ten seconds is worth about a hundred points in the 1,500 meters.

"The first two laps I was holding it right up there," Kevin said. "At this point, I had a pretty good lead. Rendon and Anderson are 1,500 meter guys. In the Paralympics in 1988, Andy was the second fastest guy in the 1,500 in the USA. That's the kind of guys I was going with there. The first two laps I hung with Andy and John and we were cruising sixteen, seventeen miles per hour. We were way ahead of the pack; some of these guys are field guys and not that fast on the track, and we were leaving their view by this time.

"By the end of the second lap, they cranked it up to eighteen miles per hour and I lost the gap on John and Andy going on the third lap. By now I was getting a little bit tired. The third lap to me is always the worst. I tried to hold it, I tried to keep my speed up to at least fifteen.

"When it came time for the gun lap, I sped back up. I always get an adrenaline rush for the final lap. I didn't let the rest of those guys gain any more ground on me. Coming down the homestretch, John and Andy had about ten seconds on me.

"They hit the finish line about the time I was into the final straightaway out of the curve. Some of the rest of the pack still had three-quarters of a lap to go. That's the kind of distance we put between us and the rest of the field. My goal was 3:50. I ran a 3:50.09. John and Andy were right at 3:40."

Kevin did some quick mental calculations. It looked like he was close to a world record.

"I felt really great, I felt that what I needed to go into Barcelona with the right mental attitude was to break that world record. It seemed like forever until they flashed the final totals on the board."

It took the race officials about three hours to total up the points and, sure enough, Kevin had broken the world record by 140 points! Dan immediately ran back to Kevin from the scorer's table and told him the news.

"I shouted 'All right!'" Kevin said. "It was a great feeling. But my first thought was that I had made the team to go to Barcelona. We kept staring at the totals and, son of a gun, William Brady was the other who guy who made it."

That afternoon, while the rest of the athletes and fans were winding down, Dan rushed to a fax machine and faxed the details of Kevin's record to Senator Dole's office in Washington D.C. Both Dan and Kevin felt that a new world record was part of their on-going effort to get Kevin named to the President's Council on Physical Fitness.

The Salt Lake City media did a long feature on Kevin and William, comparing them to the "other" major multi-athletes trying to get to Barcelona—decathletes Dan O'Brien and Dave Johnson—saying, "Now meet a couple of guys who have had that rivalry going a lot longer, Kevin and William."

Still drained from the pentathlon, Kevin competed in the various field events the following day.

"I felt pretty weak," he said, "but I did the best I could. I finished third in the shot put with a 6.17 meters, third in the discus with a 19.12, and second in the javelin with a 15.99."

The American team was to be announced Saturday night at a banquet honoring the athletes. Before the banquet, however, Kevin struck up an acquaintance with a statuesque young lady by the name of Lesley Maughn and invited her to attend as his guest.

"The banquet was real nice, everybody got dressed up, and they told about the new record holders, and finished by announcing the Barcelona team," Kevin said. "It was a pretty high day for me, although a lot of my buddies like Doug Kennedy, Bruce Cook, Jimmy Green didn't make it. There was a lot of competition—much more competition than in 1988. Everything was getting tougher. I was scared, believe me. A lot of people would be hurt if I failed! I just couldn't let all of those great people down."

But as the banquet continued to drag on, Lesley apparently grew bored and politely excused herself.

Later, in the bar in the hotel that night, Kevin came in all long-faced. All he said was, "She left." His friends couldn't help but die laughing, as he was so serious about the whole thing. They told him, "Do you blame her? After thirty photos and team meetings—she's probably got better things to do, Kevin!" A heartbroken Kevin kept saying over and over, "I just can't believe she left me, I just can't believe she left me." After a couple beers he finally lightened up a little bit, but the whole episode was a big ego-crusher for Kevin.

Lesley did call the next day, saying she'd had a bad headache and apologized about having to leave. "Those field events guys were just jealous." said Kevin.

Back in Houston, Kevin was committed to resuming his rigorous training with his coaches and the other Texas-area athletes who had qualified for the American team.

On July 24th, he and Steven flew back up to Wichita, Kansas to drive to Downs, where the town had asked Kevin to be the Grand Marshall of the parade. He stopped off in Wichita long enough to make a couple of hospital visits with the children there. Some people from Senator Dole's office were there and complimented Kevin on the way he handled the children, though they were disappointed there hadn't been better media coverage.

"The parade in Downs was super and the whole family was there, including Duane and Gerald. I stayed there several days, went to the Schoen Family reunion, got a lot of rest, and tried to heal my burn. It was pretty stubborn. I had finished all of the tons of paperwork for the President's Council on Physical Fitness and decided to mail it from Downs—for good luck. This was where it had all started, after all. I finally returned to Houston on the 29th, where I had a nice surprise waiting in the newspaper."

On July 29, 1992, *The Houston Chronicle* reported on the Houston-area team for the Paralympics, featuring Kevin and Judy Einbinder of the Southwest Wheelchair Athletic Association. The article noted that 355 American athletes would compete in Barcelona.

Also commenting was Randy Fromater, the head field-events coach of the U.S. team:

"Kevin showed me he has made significant improvement, especially in his track events (the 200 and 1,500 meters). And he came into the meet without impressive regional results."

Reporter Richard Brown quoted Fromater as saying that Kevin's toughest competition should come from Brady and Rendon.

"But my main worry was the burn," Kevin said. "It just wasn't healing. The first doctor I went to said the only thing to do was cut the ulcer out, stitch it up, and let it heal—for about fifteen hundred dollars. Since I was saving every penny to go to Barcelona, I passed. The second doctor disagreed. He said that if I got the burned area cut out and stitched up, I would have to start all over again healing a new wound. I just didn't have the luxury of that kind of time. He suggested I keep caring for it, keep training hard, and pray it healed in time to leave.

"That night, mom called and said that everyone at their church was praying for me to be healed.

"Given a choice, I'll take my chances with the people at Rose Valley Church every time. I didn't get it cut out.

"And, sure enough, it healed pretty quickly after that."

Chapter 13

The friendship between Kevin and Senator Dole continued to deepen until Dole's office invited Kevin and Dan to attend the upcoming Republican National Convention in Houston. Kevin was thrilled, partly because his hero, Arnold Schwarzenegger, a die-hard Republican *and* the best-known member of the President's Council on Physical Fitness, was among those invited to attend.

Unbeknownst to Kevin, Senator Dole had the following tribute to Kevin entered into the *Congressional Record* on Thursday July 22, 1992, from the proceedings of the legislative day of Monday July 20, 1992:

TRIBUTE TO KEVIN SAUNDERS

MR. DOLE: *Mr. President, I rise today to pay tribute to Kevin Saunders, a native Kansan and a world-class athlete, who set a new world record this past weekend in the pentathlon event at the U.S. Paralympic Trials in Salt Lake City, Utah. Kevin scored 2,249 points, shattering the existing world record.*

The pentathlon includes the shot put, javelin, discus, 1,500-meter and 200-meter races and I am proud to say that this talented Kansan will be representing the United States in Barcelona, Spain, in early September.

Paralyzed eleven years ago in a grain elevator explosion, Kevin is an inspirational young man who has overcome adversity and beaten all odds to become one of the premier athletes in the world.

When I think of determination and leadership, the name Kevin Saunders certainly comes to mind. He is truly a remarkable person and a sensational role model for America's youth.

Kevin is founder of the Wheelchair Success Fund, developed to give other wheelchair-bound individuals the support they need to contribute to their communities and reach their fullest potential. Kevin's altruism does not stop there. Even with his rigorous Olympic training schedule, Kevin has toured nationwide spreading his message of strength and hope.

As Kevin Saunders continues to reach new heights, I know my colleagues will join me in saluting him as he goes for the gold.

As word of Dole's tribute spread, Kevin's friends and family around the country swamped him with calls of congratulations and encouragement. Senator Dole had proven to be a valued friend.

In the days before the convention, Kevin continued working to improve his track and field chairs with Tim Rodwell and Tony Hernandez from Custom Controls Co. of Houston.

They took one particular version out to the University of Houston track one day and Kevin threw the javelin fifteen times before the fabricated back support bent out of position and they had to fabricate another connection for it. Back to the drawing board. The next day, they went at it again, only this time incorporating some of the elements Kevin liked about Terry Peckinpaugh's field chair. This time, it worked better, particularly in the shot put.

"I got the kind of publicity I don't like on August 6, when a biochemist and a paralyzed-skin specialist came out and took pictures of the burn on my lower back," said Kevin. "If I didn't do well in Barcelona, my butt was going to be more famous than I was!"

The next day Kevin went to visit the Texas Children's Hospital where he gave the kids some posters and one of his medals. A camera crew from Channel 2 was there and they asked him why he visited hospitalized kids so much.

Kevin's response reflected his new-found focus on effective public speaking:

"I do this because I want to give back to my community and help the kids focus on the positive and believe in themselves.

"Sometimes a crippled child will tell me, 'Kevin, I can't ever be a champion. I'll never get to go for the gold.' I'll say, 'Of course you are a champion! Everyone has a champion inside them. There's always a way to get the champion inside of you out just by trying your hardest!'"

That afternoon, he returned to Custom Controls and continued working on the balky field chair.

"I couldn't throw more than sixteen meters with the javelin or seventeen meters with the discus," Kevin said. "I wasn't ready to give up, but I wasn't happy about it, either. We kept tinkering into the night."

Finally, on the morning of the of August 8, Kevin took the re-tooled chairs back out to the University of Houston and met with Tony Hernandez of Custom Controls. He tried out two different chairs, and ended up liking his old cushion in the new chair. He also discovered that if he could hold his left knee down, it increased his distance when he threw.

Kevin studied the designs of field chairs of people like Terry Peckinpaugh, Arnold Astrada, and William Brady and noticed that if he sat with both of his legs forward and leaned back on a back cushion, he could get more *oomph* into his throws. Tony seemed intrigued by the idea and took the chairs back to the shop with that in mind.

A few days later, Tony came back with the modifications. They then took the re-tooled chair back to the track and the first time out Kevin threw about 18.5 meters. By focusing on the rhythm, rocking his head, keeping his head up, and straining to get as much rotation as possible, Kevin threw about 18.5 meters every time. Tony made some more adjustments to the chair after that. And, for the first time, Kevin began to think they were getting close.

Meanwhile, Dan had been busy in Corpus Christi arranging a fund-raising party for Kevin's trip to Barcelona. Among the sponsors was the law offices of Allison and Huerta, which sent hundreds of letters throughout South Texas:

"Dear Friends,

"On September 3, 1992, our good friend Mr. Kevin Saunders will begin competition in the 1992 Summer Paralympic Games in Barcelona, Spain. We have been a constant supporter of Kevin throughout his athletic career and believe he has the drive and determination to be the gold medal winner for the USA team. For this reason, we are inviting all our friends in the Corpus Christi Bay area to join us and Kevin on August 12, 1992 at our offices for a celebration to help support him at Barcelona. Now is the time for us to come together and help support Kevin for the tremendous amount of time and services he has given this community."

Dan started his publicity campaign back in July with newspaper ads and drummed up support. He got Media Basics and Russell Bales out of Corpus to give him a hand for free and some lawyer friends of Kevin's—Guy Allison, Steve Hastings, Albert Huerta—provided the facilities, paid for the stage, and got anything that needed to be brought in, including fencing, in preparation for the approximately two thousand people expected to show up. Among the special guests invited was Ada Jankolwitz, who was going to be the hostess. But at the very last minute, Ada couldn't come because of a medical emergency.

But most of the other invited guests came and while the total attendance figures were lower than Dan had hoped, it provided much positive publicity and created an enormous reservoir of good will.

"It was a lot of fun," Dan said, "partly because we got Gary P. Nunn to do it for a fraction of what he normally charges because he knew who Kevin was. He was in the area, and he said sure, he'd love to do it. At one point, he and Kevin sang a duet, with Kevin dancing in his chair and Gary jamming away on the guitar. The law firm of Allison & Huerta is known for its big parties."

"There were some great guys who threw the party for me," Kevin said. "That party was a lot of fun. The president of the Chamber of Commerce was there and all of these special people were there—it really meant a lot to me. I signed about three-hundred something t-shirts. The highlight for me was seeing all the people come out to support me and give their testimonials. There were hundreds and hundreds of people there. They even had the video from Salt Lake City showing all during the party on a big-screen TV."

But perhaps the most meaningful part of the evening came during the scripted and impromptu testimonials from friends far and wide.

Kevin's bankruptcy attorney Diane Sanders:

"Kevin is somebody I've been fortunate to know and I consider him one of the few uniquely great people I've had the pleasure of knowing. He's a good person, an inspiration not just to me—he inspires everybody. I wish we all had just half of his enthusiasm."

Guy Allison, who handled Kevin's lawsuits following the explosion:

"There have been times when I've asked Kevin to talk to some paraplegics and quadriplegics I represent and try and cheer them up. He's really good at that. And they really like him to come by. We tried a case in December 1992 where the lady was quadriplegic and I think the nicest thing that's happened to her since the accident four years ago was Kevin coming around."

Dr. Charles Kennedy, the surgeon who operated on him:

"You read about these things, and obviously some people do get their lives together, but it is always about somebody else, somewhere else. I've never really been involved with an individual on an on-going basis like Kevin. He's written me letters, sent me pictures. Back at our orthopedic clinic, he has a poster that he signed for us. It says, 'Thanks for your help.' No, Kevin, thanks for your help.

"We're big boosters of Kevin. And we support Kevin's bigger mission, which I think is really bigger than winning a medal at the Olympics—and that's helping kids build their lives back together after trauma. He's a role model even for kids who don't have physical problems. The whole role modeling thing is so important in today's environment. Kids are really getting the wrong messages and the wrong role models everywhere else. Here's a guy who has given a lot of his energies and a lot of his money back to people in need, because his heart is so big. Doing things like building the track in Downs, and helping people that need help in other ways, whether financially or emotionally—ways that were probably not good financial decisions on his part. But that's something he wanted to do and he did it!"

And top wheelchair athlete Randy Snow:

"I keep in touch with Kevin, both at events and on a personal level. Kevin is very motivated. He's always talking about giving 110%. He's a motivated athlete, and a very good athlete; he's very determined to succeed. Plus, you gotta like his love of people and of life. Sometimes people have accidents and they get angry, they have an attitude and they're not able to let go. They want to hold on to that attitude: 'This is not fair! Why was I dealt this hand?'

"Other people turn around and say, 'Jesus Christ! I was almost killed! I realize life can be taken from me at any moment. It could happen again so until that time I'm going to live like hell.' And that's what Kevin's done."

Although the party wasn't a big success as a fund-raiser, at that point every penny helped. Much of Dan's time was spent in raising money. Among the programs Dan created was "The Kevin Saunders Competition Fund." For making a contribution, donors received an autographed picture of Kevin in action with a small plaque that read, "Thanks for your support." That particular campaign raised about $20–25,000—mostly in the Corpus Christi Bay area.

For the various competitions in 1992, Dan and Kevin figured that they needed to raise about $80,000 towards their travel and related expenses.

After the party, Kevin returned again to Houston, both to continue training and to attend the Republican National Convention.

"Back in Houston, we also continued tinkering with the chair," Kevin said. "Pro Maxima of Houston did a great job of re-covering the seat piece, but I still wasn't happy with the feel of it. When I got home, I noticed that my burn was bleeding again. I guess the little extra seat we made on the field chair tore my scab off. It scared me a little. I wouldn't feel or notice an open, bleeding wound until I saw it—if at all. It was just something else to adjust to. Fortunately, Steven was there to dress and clean the wound—just like he was there for me all through June and July."

The next day they made sure the extra seat piece was gone.

The Republican National Convention opened August 17, 1992 and Kevin's first stop was at a press conference at the Omni Hotel, hosted by Senator Robert Dole for the Kansas delegation.

During the press conference, Senator Dole pointed at Kevin and said, "This young man right here is going to be the first disabled person in history to be appointed to the President's Council on Physical Fitness."

When his turn came to speak, Kevin made reference to Senator Dole's foresight to realize the abilities of people with disabilities and noted that disabled people have just as much right to be physically fit as everyone else. He said, "I will work hard on the President's Council on Physical Fitness to help the American people—able-bodied and disabled—to work hard and get physically fit!" The press conference went over the AP wire all over the country.

Senator Dole's office arranged for "all-access" passes for Kevin and Dan for the Convention floor—and for the many parties that were scheduled afterward.

On the convention floor, Dan was chasing down cameras, handing out press releases, and pointing people to Kevin. Dan said that ABC News in New York had Kevin on camera for at least five minutes solid while Senator Dole spoke about the ADA.

As the convention was winding down, Kevin and Dan decided to head on over toward the presidential booth area where the President, Mrs. Bush, Arnold, and all of the super-VIPs sat and watched the convention. Barbara

Bush was about seven feet from them. She kept looking down at Kevin and smiling.

"We had full view of the big screen that was behind them," Dan said. "We actually had a better position than Kevin because we could see the screen and we were face-to-face with Mrs. Bush and all of these dignitaries. NBC was dead on Kevin for another five to ten minutes, taking a lot of footage during that time."

One of Kevin's dreams from the beginning had been to meet Arnold Schwarzenegger, so he and Dan immediately fought through the crowded floor and tried to track him down. But they quickly lost him in the crush of people and eventually ended up going back to Senator Dole's suite room. At the suite, they met Judy Biviano of Senator Dole's office. Judy had been one of the primary forces behind Senator Dole's effort to get Kevin appointed to the President's Council on Physical Fitness.

"I think the most fascinating thing was not knowing Kevin and saying, 'Well, who is this guy? Is he really going to make this council?'" Judy said. "So many people want to be on it—so many famous athletes want to be on it. Magic Johnson was on it, Arnold was on it, people who were household names. Then you say, 'Who is Kevin Saunders?' And then you learn after you get to know Kevin, after you read about him and get to know him, that he's just the kind of person the council needs. More to the point, you learn being in a wheelchair doesn't mean you can't do anything; it means you can do anything if you really try."

Judy said that Senator Dole doesn't have a history of recommending anybody to anything unless he has a thorough check run on that person.

"We worked on getting Kevin on the President's Council on Physical Fitness for more than a year," she said. "We made phone calls to a lot of people in the White House, we wrote letters, we got in touch with people on the council, as well as other people who would be involved in the decision, just to get them to take a look at Kevin.

"Finally, the end product was that we were able to convince them that Senator Dole felt strongly about this and that they should take a serious look at a someone who is disabled. It was the wave of the future."

Judy said once Senator Dole reviewed the facts in Kevin's case, he simply turned to her and said, "Get it done."

"And when that happens," she said, "you go after it with vengeance. So what I had to do was be creative, and try to find those things that separated Kevin Saunders from all of the other people who wanted the appointment.

"The PCPF is a very prestigious council and we were to the point that awareness of people with disabilities was coming to a peak. And since there had never been a disabled athlete on the Council—well, hell! *everybody* wanted to be the first one! So we had to find what qualities separated Kevin Saunders from those other athletes; to find why he'd be the best choice for the President, and why the President would be proud to put his name behind it."

Judy said she believes that Senator Dole championed Kevin because he could relate with some of the experiences Kevin had suffered from when he was injured.

"After his injury, Senator Dole spent several years in a hospital recuperating. He was able to rehabilitate himself and he has great pride in that fact. He has great compassion for others who are able to do that. Someone who has excelled and achieved like Kevin has is the type of person that Bob Dole likes; someone who doesn't let a disability stand in the way—and being from Kansas was a bonus."

Kevin gratefully signed a special t-shirt he had made and gave it to Judy, who in turn gave them two more passes to the fifth floor where the V.I.P. parties were in progress. Kevin was determined not to abandon his search for Arnold.

"I wanted to give him the Austrian hiking hat I was wearing," Kevin said. "I got to the convention early and spent about $125 on Republican memorabilia to put on one side of the hat, and the other side had a bunch of pins from towns in Austria. It was my way of saying 'Thank you' to him for being an inspiration to me for physical fitness. He's gone out of his way to help a lot of disabled people, especially with the Special Olympics.

"The Austrian hiking hat is like a symbol of being physically fit. If you're wearing a hiking hat, it means you've been hiking up the side of mountains in the Alps!"

But Arnold was nowhere to be seen. Finally, Dan and Kevin dejectedly left the hotel and returned to the Astrodome. Suddenly, a large entourage cut them off. Dan shouted, "It's Arnold!"

He took off running to catch up with him, shouting "Arnold! Arnold!" But Arnold kept on walking straight ahead. So Dan screamed "Arnold!" even louder. Finally, Arnold turned his head a little bit and said, "Vat?" Dan said, "Do you want to meet Kevin Saunders?" Arnold is walking all the time and not even slowing down and says, "I've already met Kevin Saunders." Dan says, "No, no! I mean, Kevin Saunders the wheelchair athlete!"

Arnold kept walking, but said, "Is he here?" And Dan said, "He's right behind you!" Kevin, who had been following them as best he could, weaving in and out among hundreds of people in the hallways, was right there.

Arnold stopped, turned around, and stuck out his hand and said, "I know you. You're the man that is trying to get on the President's Council for Physical Fitness. How are you doing?" Kevin replied that he was fine and offered Arnold the hiking hat, asking him if he knew what it was. He said, "Yes, it is a hiking hat from my home country of Austria. Are you sure you vant me to haff it?" Kevin insisted, adding what an inspiration he thought Arnold had been to him and millions of other Americans. Arnold replied, "Vell, thank you. I vill look forvard to vorking mit you on the President's Council for Physical Fitness. OK? OK!"

Arnold then smiled at Kevin, tossed him a t-shirt, whirled and strode purposefully out of the building, his giant entourage moving in concert, like a flock of birds.

Still dazed, Kevin and Dan turned and gave each other enthusiastic "high-fives" and shouted like little kids.

The two finally wandered back to Senator Dole's party.

"Once there, I got to talk to both the Senator and Elizabeth Dole. I was real proud that Senator Dole was working hard for me and that he wanted me to have that appointment to the President's Council on Physical Fitness—and I told them so."

Chapter 14

As much fun as he'd had at the Republican National Convention, Kevin was anxious to resume training. Some publications had already tabbed him as the favorite to win the gold in the pentathlon because he was the current world record holder. And, despite losing a few days hobnobbing with Legislators and Terminators, Kevin agreed with that assessment.

"I felt that I should win the gold medal in Barcelona," he said. "I didn't see any reason then why I shouldn't. Everything was going very well. You just have to focus, get the job done, and not let all the hoopla get to you. I just went over and over in my head what I had to do to get that gold medal—and then get back home.

"But as it got closer, I started thinking 'How can I do this?' It's pretty stressful sometimes because you're setting goals, dealing with the unknown, and you're under pressure to perform. So with your training and your traveling, it's a high-pressure lifestyle, even for your average wheelchair guy. There was an extreme amount of pressure for me as world champion to win that gold medal."

Unlike at Seoul, Kevin didn't recognize many of the names of the listed competitors—beyond William Brady and Rudi Van Den Abbeele and a couple of the Europeans—for the Barcelona Games. That, naturally, created more stress.

"Finally, when we arrived in Barcelona, there was a lot of head games going on. A guy came up to me in Barcelona and said, 'I've run a three minute and forty second 1,500 meter.' I didn't know whether he could or not; he was just trying to mess with my mind. He wanted me to *think* he could, so I'd get nervous. He wanted me to think, 'Gosh! If he can run that fast...' So I didn't pay any attention to him because I've had guys do that before. I've done it too—ask Rudy—that's just part of athletics."

When time came for Kevin to fly to Barcelona courtesy of Delta Airlines, he was joined by Dan and their roommate Kent Oliver. They were joined by the head coach of the U.S. wheelchair division, Terry Jessup of Mesquite, Texas, and more than 350 American athletes.

The 1992 Paralympic Games in Seoul drew five thousand athletes and seven thousand volunteers for the twelve sports. As before, events were held according to the degree of the disability in the wheelchair, along with categories for people with cerebral palsy, the visually impaired, and amputee divisions.

The eleven-day Paralympics proved to be extremely popular in Spain. The five track-and-field days drew about fifty thousand fans each day. Additionally, each day of the Paralympics—September 3–13—was televised ten to twelve hours daily by Spanish television stations.

The Paralympics was dubbed by one observer as "the poor man's Olympics" because many people attended who could not afford to go to the event's more expensive counterpart.

Terry, Kevin, Kent, and Dan retained some vivid images from the Paralympics, images that would last a lifetime: Kevin's friend, Tony Volpentest, with little below his knees and elbows running the 100 meters in 11.63 seconds and the 200 meters in 23.07 seconds, breaking both world records. A Nigerian without a shoulder and an arm running a 10.60 in the 100. A blind sprinter setting a world record, nearly running away from his sighted guide.

Dan had a unique perspective of the games. He served as a volunteer-backup photographer to the official American Paralympic photographer, which gave him (and his assistant Kent) virtually unlimited access to the performance fields.

Not that everything was perfect in Spain. There were a number of angry athletes when several wheelchairs were left behind on the overcrowded charter flight. The four-thousand-dollar, custom chairs arrived just in time for competition, but not in time for practice runs. Kevin's chairs, fortunately, had arrived on time and intact.

Kevin had flown from Houston, straight to Barcelona three days before the Games and stayed in the same Olympic Village the Olympic athletes had stayed in. There was an American compound and Kevin knew a lot of the American athletes—Cisco Jeter, Tom Cellars, Mike Ward, and Brad Ramadge.

"The opening ceremonies on September 3 were really a tremendous thing; they were even better, most people said, than the ceremonies for the regular Olympics. The guy shot the arrow in the torch like before. It was spectacular.

"They had some tremendous people with disabilities there. There was one guy there they said had the IQ of Einstein, but could hardly move anything, just a finger or two on one hand. He types with his computer and his computer talks it all out with a computer-voice. And he was just one of hundreds."

It was Dan's first Paralympics. "It was an incredible spectacle and size that, according to what the other athletes told me, was grander in scale than anything that had been done before—it was massive, it was just as big and impressive as the Olympics. In fact, two of the nights they had riot police fighting off crowds trying to get into the stadium, and that didn't even happen during the Olympics.

"It was a good feeling to see that on a global scale, people are warming to the idea that this is really exciting, seeing these guys in chariots going around a track, or watching a guy with one leg sprinting across the 100-yard dash in world record time. It was a life-changing experience for me as a spectator."

Unfortunately for Kevin, the pentathlon was not held until September 10, meaning that he had to wait nearly ten days to compete.

"I was pumped up, I was so ripped to get at it, but it was a long wait," Kevin said. "I tried every day to keep my focus, to mentally and visually go over and over what

I had to do. I read from a Bible a girl gave me and the other competitors. I tried to keep my faith and not lose my edge."

But it wasn't long before the waiting began to take its toll on Kevin. "Kevin's not the type of person who likes to sit still, Dan said. He likes to go full steam ahead, so the waiting really affected him in terms of focus. Kevin's whole life revolves around staying focused and hitting the mark. Waiting wasn't easy for him."

"I'd go down to the track each day, and I'd be really stoked," Kevin said, "because when I first got on the track, I was running with two guys who were really fast— Tom Sellars from Florida and Kenny Carnes from Maryland. Also running well were Scott Hallenback and Joe Tadisco, and I was hammering right with them—we were going like 19.6 MPH. And on the track, that's *moving*. For me, a pentathlete, to be running with the guys who run the exhibition 1,500 meters—and they're the fastest guys there are—felt fantastic.

Unfortunately, during practice Kevin collided with another athlete and bent the front wheel and steering of his racing chair. Fortunately, Chris Peterson, a chair designer from Top End was in Barcelona and could fix it.

While he was waiting on the repair, Kevin went to the beaches near Barcelona, but more often he found himself tooling around the Olympic Village, the practice track, and even the competition track, alone, trying to maintain his focus.

"I tried to relax, to *believe* I was going to win that gold medal," Kevin said. "I think that as long as I ended up waiting I might have lost a little focus. You can always look back and say you could have done this or that. I was in good shape, but I think that more important than staying in shape, is staying in focus."

Seoul was the first time Kevin had participated in a major international competition, and all he had expected of himself was to do his best. When he won the bronze medal it was a complete surprise to him. But after he had established himself for three years as the world's record holder, he knew he was only two steps away from the gold medal. So, once Kevin finally got to Barcelona, he was really feeling the pressure in a profound way. "When I said my prayers, I asked God to please let me give my very best, to have the strength, the power, the endurance, and the will to win."

Kevin had to deal with his stress alone during the days leading up to the Games. Because he was in the residence quarters of the Olympic Village, media representatives—like Dan and Kent—were strictly prohibited.

"They didn't want people interrupting the focus of athletes," Dan said. "The last thing they want to do is have journalists and photographers in the residence area, so we rarely even saw Kevin after we arrived. Other than when he was on the field, we saw him maybe four times during the entire two weeks. He had to do it himself."

There were other problems as well. A nasty flu bug was sweeping the Olympic Village. A number of athletes didn't adapt to the food and water. Still others were waiting on their wheelchairs up until the last moment.

"After about a week, I had a sore throat, something of a temperature, and some sniffles," Kevin said. "I couldn't sleep either."

Kevin went to bed early the night before the pentathlon and arose early—this was one race he didn't want to miss.

"In the hours before the beginning of the pentathlon, I mostly rested and did a lot of mental visualization, seeing myself on the winner's stand," Kevin said. "I broke down each event in my mind:

"Shot put—deep breath, explosion, full rotation, and wrist snap. Get mad! Keep chest and head up.

"Javelin—make sure I'm balanced, violent left arm, whip arm with the javelin, roll off finger tips.

"200 meters—explode with the gun, fast hands, fast, fast, fast, then start to stroke hard, hard, hard on the straightaway with high and hard strokes.

"Discus—relax, rotation, when shoulder locks out—explode, follow through, go after it.

"1,500 meters—start fast, get up to nineteen miles per hour, then slow stroke down and explode through the push rim, just concentrate on high elbows with a slow, hard stroke. Pick up the pace on the third lap.

"I could just see it! I could *see* it!"

As always, the shot put was the first event.

"I was so stoked and ready to get that shot put I could hardly stand it," Kevin said. "I wanted to have the adrenaline of a mother who lifts a car off her trapped baby! I tried to create that same adrenaline flow in my body—I was just ready to fly out of that chair."

In the minutes before Kevin threw, he again reviewed all of the mechanics of it: the deep breath, the high elbow, the hard pull with the left arm. Then coming around with the chest up, picking a spot out and driving the shot put up and out as far as you can.

"At the same time I was thinking, 'Oh my God, my baby's under the car!'—and I've got to put that same kind of force into this shot put."

And that's exactly what Kevin did. With a grunt that could be heard in the stands, Kevin strained and grimaced and threw the shot more than seven meters—which would have placed him in contention with the athletes who *only* threw the shot.

"I threw it further than I've *ever* thrown it before, by a long way," Kevin said, "and that's my weakest event too. I mean I was *excited!*"

A wave of adrenaline washed over Kevin and several of the pentathletes surged forward to congratulate him. It was the throw of the day.

Suddenly, the English judge at the shot put walked up, waving her arms emphatically, holding up a red flag. Kevin's throw was disqualified. She said he'd pulled the shot from his cheek too soon, too far. The throw didn't count.

"I figured there must be some kind of mistake, so I appealed to the head judge. I said, 'When you're paralyzed and you're pulling with your left arm so hard, your head will just naturally pull away a little bit. I think there's something wrong with the rule. If that's how we're judging here, then I think you need to be open to the possibility that there needs to be some modification of the rules.'"

But the head field judge, who spoke only fractured English, dismissed Kevin's appeal.

Still rattled, Kevin concentrated on getting a distance with his second throw.

Instead of focusing on sheer force, Kevin focused on sticking the shot to his chin like it had glue on it and pushing it out, exactly according to the rules. He lost a meter in distance, 150 points, but Kevin didn't want the same thing to befall him that happened to Dan O'Brien in New Orleans in the pole vault. "If you don't mark, if you end up getting three red flags, you're out of there before you even get started! So I had to go just to get the mark on the second throw. It was 6.04 meters.

"So with the third throw, I went to crank it again. I put the stuff on it, just like I'd done the first time. I was stoked when I let it fly. I went all out again; I put maximum force behind that lead ball.

"And I got red flagged again."

The second call was even more questionable than the first. This time the entire American coaching contingent howled in protest—to no avail.

"At this point, I'm in sixteenth place, out of twenty-one competitors, with 681 points," Kevin said. "For instance, Mohammad Sadeghi threw the shot 9.02 meters and had 861 points. I'm way behind, I've got some ground to make up. A lot of guys are beating me. I don't like to be that far down."

The only consolation for the American team was that Brady had a good throw: 7.18 meters, which was good for 854 points.

As the other competitors threw, Kevin tried desperately to calm himself. He silently raged at the judge for a time, then attempted to gather the fractured pieces of his concentration. But the focus wouldn't come. He kept returning, over and over again, back to the shot put.

"I'd think, 'This lady cost me the gold medal,'" Kevin said, "then I realized that I couldn't think like that. It was really me, I had to look inside myself for what it took to win. I couldn't blame someone else. I had to focus. But still some negative thoughts got through.

"I felt let-down because I'd worked so hard, I'd prayed so hard to do my very best and now I had a meter taken away from me. I just couldn't understand why. I throw like that all the time. But this time one judge felt it was beyond the rules.

"Finally, I managed to focus. I had to go for it. I couldn't change what had happened, so I had to deal with reality. I had to put the shot totally out of my mind. I had to focus on the next event—the javelin."

But the javelin throw brought its own pressures. Kevin now had precious margin for error. Even an average throw would eliminate him from medal competition.

"I knew I couldn't afford any mistakes because I was so far behind," Kevin said. "I had to try to work my way up. So again, I broke it down into the mechanics—tried to whip my right arm, pull hard with my left arm to initiate the throw, and make my arm whip like Indiana Jones cracking that whip in the movies—and go out after it."

Kevin's third throw was the best—18.06 meters, worth 702 points. The 702 points allowed him to rise somewhat in the standings.

"But Brady threw the personal record of his life in the javelin!" Kevin said. "He threw it 21.78 meters, which gave him another 886 points. So after two events, he's #1. I was happy for him. It was a great performance. But that's what great athletes must do—they must rise to the occasion in the Olympic Games."

The last event before lunch was the 200 meters. Because of the number of athletes, the event was held in heats.

Kevin was in the first heat and finished second. His time was 31.54 seconds—OK, but it wasn't super. It was worth 1,007 points. Jose Abal of Spain ran it in 29.53 seconds and picked up 1,063 points. It wasn't the fastest Kevin had ever run, but there was a head wind blowing across the track. However, Kevin wasn't too disappointed with the time because it brought him all the way up to fifth place.

For the first time, Kevin began to dare to hope that he again had a chance at the gold medal.

"My only shot was to crank the discus as hard as I could," he said. "You want to throw the discus the same way a clay trap comes out of a loader: You've got to get that arm rotated all of the way back as far as you can rotate, until your shoulder sort of locks out as far it will go, then you've just got to whip it around. You also want to get a good plane on it, especially when the wind is blowing in your face, because if you get the proper plane on it, the discus will actually rise and go further."

Kevin again threw below his personal best, but better than the bulk of the field. The best throw traveled 19.48 meters, good for 850 points. Maurizio Nalin of Italy picked up 1,078 points with a throw of 28.46 meters. Vojtech Vasicek of Czechoslovakia threw the discus 21.80 meters for 978 points.

As always, the gold medal was to be decided with the 1,500 meters.

Luckily, Kevin was in the heat with the competitors ahead of him at that point: Vasicek of Czechoslovakia, Abal of Spain, Nalin of Italy, and Rudi Van Den Abbeele (the Frenchman who had won the gold in Seoul and was the world record holder before Kevin). There were twelve competitors in each heat and ten lanes on the track, so they stacked the racers all of the way across. They even stacked two racers, who were way down in the point standings, behind the front line. Kevin was in lane four.

By now it was 8:30 p.m. and 50,000 people still packed the stands as they'd done virtually every night of the Games.

When the gun fired, Kevin knew he had to get out as quickly as possible. He didn't want to get hung up with the slower runners. "Pretty soon it was just me, Vasicek, and Abal—and brother, we were crankin!'" recalls Kevin. "People were screaming because there was a guy from Spain in the race.

"When I felt they weren't pressing the pace enough, I kicked it up because I knew that in the heat before us, 3:48 had won. So I knew we had to press the pace. I didn't want somebody to come up from behind to pass where I already was in the standings. So whenever Abal would slow down, I'd whip alongside of him and try to push the pace. We were going seventeen to eighteen, sometimes nineteen or more miles per hour. We were hammerin', we were blazin', people were just screaming. My head wanted to get dizzy from the noise and the adrenaline."

Going into the beginning of the fourth lap, Kevin decided to make his move to pass the other two. By then, there was a big gap between the leaders and the rest of the pack. The gold medal was on the line. Kevin knew he had to win to get the gold medal. The others knew it too.

"I couldn't even feel fatigue! I was hammering and hammering going for all I was worth. The noise of the screaming got louder and my head was spinning faster, everybody was going wild. So I tried to make my move.

"I pulled up alongside the Spaniard and was going to pass him and as I did, he moved out a little bit and our arms got caught. They showed that on the big TV screen monitors in the stadium and the people must have thought that I grabbed his arm or something and forty thousand people started booing and whistling at me! I hesitated momentarily because I'd already been red flagged on my shot put. I thought, 'Wow, the last thing I need is to get disqualified when I'm running this last race!' So I slowed down and pulled in behind him."

Just as Kevin slowed, Vojtech swerved in front of Kevin and boxed him in coming around the last curve!

"I slowed a little more, then tried to go way around the outside of Vojtech to pass him," Kevin said. "I strained until I thought my heart would burst and actually made up several feet. But I couldn't get out there fast enough in time to do anything.

"We hit the finish line *blam! blam! blam!*"

On tape, the finish is just a blur. But stop action

photography revealed Vojtech first by a fraction, Jose second, with Kevin finishing third—all within the same second.

Vojtech was credited with a 3:42.02 for 1,090 points, Jose was listed at 3:42.04 for 1,090 points, and Kevin was credited with a 3:42.47 for 1,086 points.

It was several minutes before the officials scores—and standings—were flashed on the scoreboard at the end of the stadium.

But Dan and Kent had been keeping their own totals—and the results didn't look good.

"I was kind of sad, but I was relieved because we'd worked so hard to get there and I was a little glad it was over," Dan said. "When he placed third in the 1,500, I was afraid that that might not even be enough for him to win a bronze."

"I can't describe the feelings I had while I was staring at the gigantic JumboTron screen waiting for the official results and final standings," Kevin said. "It was the longest five to ten minutes of my life. I didn't want to blink, it was so intense."

The totals came to Vojtech with 4,345 points, Jose with 4,339 points, and Kevin with 4,326 points—just nineteen points behind Vojtech.

And that's the way the medals were awarded. Vojtech was also credited with a new world record.

"When I saw Kevin had won the bronze medal, all this, almost two years, just whooshed out of my body," Dan said. "I was floating I was so relieved it was all over. Then almost immediately, I was really worried about how Kevin was gonna feel because he was so sure that he was going to win the gold medal—there was no doubt in his mind."

"Afterwards, he was just out of it; Kevin was completely gone. He was fried for days."

Kevin had lost the gold medal by 0.42 of a second.

Or fourteen centimeters in the shot put.

"All I could think was 'I *threw* the shot put that far!'" Kevin said. "Mine went there! It was there! The only problem was, that judge flagged me on a judgment call. I'm not saying *if—mine was there!* I think that's a little bit different that the guys who keep saying, 'If only I'd done this or that...' I threw it! But that was the judgment at the time. And I respect that.

"Picking up the medal, I knew how bad I thought I needed that gold medal, how I thought it was so important to everything. And how I didn't get it. In Seoul, I was just so elated because I never thought I'd get anything. I was so happy. In one way I was happy in Barcelona, because I got a medal. But in another way, I was heartbroken because I thought I needed the gold for all of the rest of my goals to come true. I'd been the world champion, I'd been the world record holder for three years. I knew I needed it. It hurts when you're so close and you so *easily* could have won the gold medal. But it wasn't to be."

There were other disappointments. William Brady finished in sixth place with 4,175 points.

"I was in first place after four events in Barcelona," William recalled, "but I knew these guys were really fast on the track and that's not really my forte. So I was just trying to hang on, so to speak. Kevin felt for a time that it was hopeless to win the gold medal. But it turned out that I went all of the way from first to sixth place and Kevin jumped all of the way from sixteenth to third place! So he got the bronze medal again!"

There were other interesting facets to the pentathlon. Jose, the Spanish silver medalist, incidentally, was ambulatory. After the medal ceremony, he got out of his wheelchair and walked to a waiting crowd of family and friends.

"That's fine by me," Kevin said. "As long as he has a medical reason to have a wheelchair, I don't care if he has full use of his arms and legs. I want to compete against anyone who wants to go for it in a wheelchair. I like competition. Walking doesn't help you all of that much in a racing wheelchair once you sit down."

The field events are weighted according to the level of a person's disability. In each event, the balance factor is taken into consideration in awarding points. Each athlete throws against their own world records set by the class of disability. For example, in the discus, Jose threw 28.16 meters and was given 764 points. Kevin only threw 19.48 meters, but was awarded 850 points. Only the track events aren't weighted.

Kevin tried to stay interested in the other events over the final few days, but had to fight a growing depression. He did support his roommates Tom and Cisco, who along with Mike Knoll and Scott Hollenbeck, won the gold in the 4 x 100 relay.

"I was really happy for them," Kevin said. "The closing ceremonies were four days later, on the 14th. I stayed to the end. After the medal ceremony, I went out and celebrated a little bit with Dan and Kent. I'd hardly been out of the Village until that night. We talked it all over.

"I decided I had to look at it like I'd could have missed out on *any* medal. I was still really depressed about it. I really needed that medal—or so I thought—it really was a missing piece of the puzzle.

"Then somewhere in the evening, while eating Spanish food and talking with good friends, I discovered that I liked winning, but I liked winning friends even more. After it was all said and done, and you had to choose between friends and gold medals, what would you still want years later? Would you rather have people who love and respect you or would you rather have a gold medal? The gold medal is just something to give you exposure; it's a goal to be reached. But it is not an end in itself. It can't be. It's a means. It's a means to get something out of life that we want. It's not an end. You've got to take that medal, take that championship, and do something with it.

"And that's what I vowed to do."

Chapter 15

"When I finally got back to Houston, I met a few buddies and we went out and celebrated again to relax, unpack, unwind, and to cut through the jet lag," Kevin said.

"The next morning, I met with Steven. He knew the whole story, how I lost the gold by four-tenths of a second. When I saw him, I had tears in my eyes. I knew what he'd given up that summer to help me. And I'd told him over and over again, 'If you work hard and never give up, you can do anything.' So I really felt bad that I'd lost that gold medal.

"When he came up, I shyly put the bronze medal in his hand.

"'Dad,' he shouted, 'this is awesome! You got one! Look at this: this is an entire summer—right here! Man!'

"I said, 'Son, I'm sorry I didn't win that gold medal.'

"Steven said, 'Yeah, dad—but you got one! Just think if you'd only gotten fourth place. How would you have talked your way out of *that* one?'"

Within a couple of days of leaving the heady atmosphere of Barcelona, Kevin was back to working out in Corpus Christi gyms and putting in anonymous miles on the track and city back roads.

"I was working out by myself in the gym when I had something of a revelation," Kevin said. "I realized that in a lot of phases of my life, I had used the accident as an excuse, that somehow I was no longer responsible for my actions. I saw that my single-minded obsession with the gold was just another way of not wanting to grow up. I wanted to stay a happy-go-lucky kid, a kid with blonde hair from Kansas. And if I drank too much, or let someone down, hey! I didn't mean anything by it.

"But as I worked on my triceps that day, I think I began to understand, maybe for the first time, that accident, this wheelchair—none of that changes anything. I'm still responsible for what I do, for who I am. Maybe it was time to grow up, to get past the pain.

"Maybe it took losing the gold in Barcelona to make me realize what's really important."

Shortly after returning to the United States, Dan arranged another speaking tour with the power company that would take him to forty different schools, mostly in Houston and Corpus.

Also since Barcelona, Kevin and Dan had given little thought to being named to the President's Council on Physical Fitness. Without the gold medal, Kevin felt like the Council was now only a distant dream.

But on October 6, 1992, that dream became a reality.

More than a year's hard work by Senator Dole and his staff had finally paid off. Kevin was notified the day before that there was to be an official announcement at a press conference at the Marriott West Loop in Houston.

At that time, Kevin Saunders, formerly of Downs, Kansas, was going to be appointed as the first physically challenged member of the President's Council on Physical Fitness.

"It was an amazing, amazing day," Kevin said. "I was so stoked, I could hardly stand it waiting for the press conference. I'd planned to get my hair cut that day, short like my mom likes it, and she called three times to remind me to do it!"

While eagerly waiting for the first meeting of the President's Council, Kevin tried to stay busy speaking in schools and staying in shape for upcoming meets.

Meanwhile, in Downs, nearly fifty local businesses, schools, churches, and municipal organizations took out a full-page advertisement in *The Downs News & Times* on October 15, with a giant headline that read: "Congratulations to Kevin Saunders, your home town is proud of you." Also featured in the advertisement was a picture of Kevin receiving his medal and Kevin's first-person account of the different events during the pentathlon. He ended the article with this sentence: "The friendship and support that all of you have given me means much more than a gold medal ever could."

On November 20, 1992, Kevin was invited to attend Kansas State University's homecoming. Coach Bill Snyder asked him to come into the football team's locker room and make a few remarks to the team. Kevin, in an unusual loss for words, said simply, "Don't ever ever quit, believe in your hearts that you can win because there's always a way—now go out and stomp the Cowboys!" Later, he flipped the coin at midfield to start the game. KSU beat Oklahoma State that day, 10–0. Afterwards, the team signed the game ball and gave it to him.

Bill Snyder had high praise for Kevin, as did many of the Kansas State athletes. Scott Scroggins said, "It was a great experience for the football team to interact with somebody with that level of perseverance. None of them will ever forget it."

After the game, Kevin drove back to Downs.

"Everybody treated me royally that day," Kevin said. "Even dad, who doesn't say much, was pretty proud.

"I told them, 'My pursuit isn't the pursuit of wealth, but to change the way people perceive things. I believe the American dream is open to everyone, regardless of whether they're in a chair or not.

"From the time I was hurt, I wanted to create someone like a James Bond character in a wheelchair so kids in chairs could say, 'Hey! I want to grow up and do that!' That concept could put a smile on a lot of people's faces.

"And being named as the first disabled person on the President's Council on Physical Fitness has sure put a smile on mine!"

There had initially been some speculation that there would be a ceremony to commemorate Kevin's election to the Council, but the executive director of the President's Council on Physical Fitness, Capt. John Butterfield, said that the PCPF had never previously hosted a ceremony to honor new members.

"I didn't want a ceremony just for me, but for the 42 million people in America with disabilities," Kevin said. "They need to know that people in Washington D.C. care, that there's somebody who knows that fitness is linked to your health. There's a distinct correlation there.

"But I didn't want any special treatment either. I was just too pumped about the first Council meeting January 9–10, 1993, in Washington D.C."

The quarterly meeting of the Council was to be held at the Washington Westin Hotel—on a weekend because Arnold Schwarzenegger was in the middle of filming his latest movie. When the time came, Kevin decided he'd take Dan and another friend, Fritz Fischer.

One of the last things Kevin did before leaving Houston was contact Mary Lou Retton's office. He had heard that she felt like she hadn't been treated well by the President's Council on Physical Fitness. In fact, he had been told that he had been given Mary Lou Retton's appointment. She had been serving in an advisory capacity in the past. Kevin felt bad about that as she had been a great inspiration to him because of all she had achieved as an athlete.

Mary Lou's husband, Shannon Kelly, assured Kevin that they weren't mad at him, just at the council in Washington. Shannon said that Mary Lou had already done a lot of work for the Council, speaking around the country and appearing at various events for them, and that Arnold had corresponded with Mary Lou, to the effect, that she was going to get the appointment to the Council that had gone to Kevin instead. Kevin was worried that some people could make a legitimate argument that Mary Lou deserved the appointment more. But Shannon indicated that there was a lot of deadweight on the council, people who hadn't been to one meeting in four years. He thought they should be replaced with people with who were going to be active."

As usual, Kevin threw himself into preparation for the weekend with the same single-minded devotion with which he attacked most problems.

First, he read all of the magazine and newspaper articles he could find on Arnold, read his unauthorized biography by Wendy Leigh, as well as his fitness books, read the book on him that was done by a photographer, did his daily workouts like Arnold, and watched all of his videos—he was ready for Arnold!

"The main reason I'd wanted to get on the Council, ever since President Bush suggested that I be put on it, has always been to promote fitness. But it didn't hurt that it also turned out that the appointment would give me the opportunity to meet Arnold; I didn't want to let it pass by.

"After I'd done all that reading and viewing about Arnold, I asked famed bodybuilder Lee LaBrada what I should talk about with Arnold. He said, 'Just be yourself when you talk to him.' Other people said, 'Be sure and stand up for yourself, show him that you know what to do, that you're someone who'll get in there and do your best.'

"Finally, I went to the Austrian consulate in Houston with a tape recorder and asked them to help me correctly say a phrase in Austrian German: 'Together we will crush the enemies of health and fitness—let's do it!' Then I wrote that on a real cool sheet of paper and signed it to give to him."

Between watching *Terminator* and *Kindergarten Kop*, Kevin also read everything he could find on the President's Council on Physical Fitness. When the time finally came to leave, he felt prepared for any and every challenge—or question—he might encounter in Washington D.C.

Kevin, Dan, and Fritz flew out of Houston at 8:00 a.m. and arrived at the hotel just thirty minutes before the opening 1:00 p.m. meeting. Even though Arnold didn't attend the opening session, Kevin hung on every word.

"I got to the meeting of the executive council, the directors, and some of advisors just in time," Kevin said. "When they asked me to introduce myself and tell them a little bit about myself, I told them that I was a wheelchair athlete and that I had a tremendous hunger and desire to make physical fitness something for everyone.

"I said, 'I know what I want in life and I'm not afraid to go through a crowded place or to the top of a flight of stairs if there is something I want that's worth getting at the top of those stairs. Some people aren't like that. They let society and the way people look at them restrict what they do in life. My desire and my drive are to change the way people see other people with disabilities.

"I said, 'People can do anything; you might be surprised at what people can do.'"

In the course of a ten-minute introduction, Kevin also briefly recounted his life since the grain elevator explosion.

After his talk, the council's vice-chairman, Suzanne Timpken of Canton, Ohio, rushed up and asked Kevin if he'd ever considered a career as a motivational speaker: "If you haven't, you should! You're great!"

The rest of the meeting was standard Council business, but Kevin attended every detail with keen interest. He also met Dr. Kenneth Cooper, another advisor to the President's Council, and the country's premiere health and fitness expert.

"I told him that he was the guy we all cussed under our breath while we were doing those twelve-minute runs in college!" Kevin said. "Fortunately, he's a good sport— he understood."

At 7:00 p.m., Arnold sponsored a reception and dinner for the Council at the hotel, complete with a chamber trio in tuxedoes playing Austrian music.

Though there are only twenty people on the President's Council, about forty people showed up at the reception. Kevin was joined by his cousin Leah Buikstra, Fritz, and Dan.

One of the first people Kevin met was Sammy Lee, the first Asian-American on the President's Council on Physical Fitness. Sammy Lee was the first Asian-American to win an Olympic Gold medal. Kevin also met Franco Columbo, the Italian boxer and body-builder who first came to America with Arnold and later became Mr. Olympia and Mr. Universe. A little later he met Joe Weider, the muscle and fitness expert from whom Kevin had learned so many great tips on working out. Joe saw Kevin's brochure with the photograph of the rip on his body in the shot put, and said he wanted to do a special feature on Kevin in his magazine, *Muscle & Fitness*.

Toward the end of the reception, Kevin was introduced to Sergeant Shriver and Eunice Kennedy Shriver.

"Mr. Shriver told me I was a remarkable young man and he asked me what I attributed my success to," Kevin said. "I said it was growing up on a farm in Kansas, learning good values, developing a good work ethic—and eating fresh vegetables and home-cooking everyday. He said, 'I grew up on a farm, too! I ate those good vegetables and all of mom's home-made cooking, too! That should have made me strong too—but look at all I got.' He held up one skinny arm.

"He then got down on one knee and we talked a while—he's a great guy and we got to joking around back and forth and we had a great time."

Later Capt. Butterfield's wife told Kevin that Corpus Christi was one of the thirteen different places they'd been stationed at during her husband's career, and that the people there were the friendliest of any place they'd ever lived. She said it was the only place they cried over when they had to leave all their friends.

Just before dinner, Kevin saw Arnold working his way toward him through the crowd.

"He was the complete diplomat, saying hello, shaking hands with everybody along the way; he was very professional—and very aloof," Kevin said. "When he came to me, I said, 'I know who you are,' in a heavy Austrian accent before Arnold said anything. It was the same thing he said to me in Houston at the Convention. Dan and everybody was horrified. Arnold just stood there looking at me for a moment.

"After a long pause, I told him that it was fate that had brought me there: 'It's destiny, Arnold.' I guess that was kind of bold, too.

"Anyway, I pressed ahead. I introduced Arnold to Leah and told him what a great athlete she was, then I told him what I'd learned in German with an Austrian accent, and gave him the paper it was written on. He looked at it and read it. Arnold didn't say a whole lot. He was probably pretty taken aback by the whole thing.

"I guess I wasn't making much of an impression."

Not surprisingly, Arnold's dinner was *trés* elegant as well. Kevin, Dan, Fritz and Leah sat at a table with the Jane Blaylock family. Jane is another member of the Council.

After dinner, Kevin continued to introduce himself around the room. Among the people he talked with were Keith Barish, the Hollywood producer who put together the Planet Hollywood concept with Arnold; promoter Jim Lormer; Dr. Cory Servass, editor of *The Saturday Evening Post;* and Mr. and Mrs. Richard Cremers, well-known Texas ranchers from Kerrville, Texas.

"The highlight of the evening was the awarding of the Distinguished Service Awards by the President's Council on Physical Fitness," Kevin said. "Arnold, of course, handed them out. When they called my name, I went up and Arnold got down on one knee and smiled at me. I told him that I didn't feel I had done anything to deserve this award yet.

"He said, 'You've visited a lot of schools, you've done a lot of things to raise the awareness of fitness and health to all Americans.'

"I said, 'Thank you. You've been a great inspiration to me. And I think the world of you.'

Council meetings began early the next morning. For the first session, Kevin sat with Dr. Don Cooper from Oklahoma State University.

"I tried to concentrate on really seeing and looking at what was going on around me," Kevin said. "I know that in life, many people listen, but few people hear." Kevin listened to a number of professional groups put on different presentations, including: James Herold, deputy director of Health Promotion and Disease Prevention, and representatives from the Minority Health Institute, from the Native American Youth Initiative, from Operation

First Choice, from the National 4-H Clubs, from the Silver Eagle Corps, the AMA, Workcare, the Private Sector Initiative—and so many others. He heard the Chairman's report, the Vice Chairman's Report, and an update on the "Ask Arnold" program.

The afternoon was filled with more meetings, more reports, more media campaigns and proposed videos.

"I saw a whole bunch of ways I could fit in and have a positive impact for the Council," Kevin said. "I could tour the country for the PCPF with the goal of getting people interested in physical fitness. There's no telling what we could do if we targeted fitness and health, illustrated by some of the things I can do in a wheelchair. The results would probably be phenomenal."

Between the presentations, Kevin huddled with Dan and the others who critiqued his impromptu meetings with Arnold. Dan in particular wasn't ready to pass out any high marks.

"Finally, I got Arnold off to one side and told him about doing one-armed chin ups and the backward somersault in the wheelchair and how a bunch of mothers came up and said how that had inspired their able-bodied kids to get into shape," Kevin said.

"For the first time, Arnold laughed and said, 'That's great. How are you able to do the one-armed chin up? That is one thing I could never do.' I said, 'It took a lot of hard work—as I'm sure you know—and my skinny legs helped.'"

At the final afternoon meeting, Arnold formally introduced Kevin and the other new member, Harris Frank, to the entire Council. Arnold spent nearly five minutes recounting Kevin's life story and praising his courage:

"Arnold said, 'Despite being handicapped'—and he used the word 'handicapped'—not aware that the word is no longer politically correct in most circles—'Kevin will bring a new dimension to the Council. It is long overdue. And I am real excited about the prospect of having Kevin here.'

"When I was asked to speak, I said it was a real thrill

for me just to be there: 'Arnold, you can identify with this—this is the biggest honor in my lifetime, the biggest honor I've ever received. And I'm grateful to the people in Washington D.C., to President Bush, to Senator Dole, and the people who cared enough about *all* people in America, who had the vision and the foresight, to appoint someone in a wheelchair to the President's Council on Physical Fitness. That shows America that they really do care in Washington—and that they want to make physical fitness and health a priority for everyone.

"I said, 'Health and fitness enabled me to be a survivor. I am now mentally and physically fit and ready to take on the world. It is like John F. Kennedy said: 'Physical fitness is the first step to all other forms of excellence.' Get those people out of their homes using health and fitness for an enjoyable, happy lifestyle!

"I set a goal a couple years ago to get on this Council. It took a lot of hard work and I never gave up hope. Thank you for that opportunity."

After the final session, Kevin helped Dr. Cory Servass carry her bags to her car. Cory said she'd been much impressed with Kevin and his presentation and invited him to attend the Indianapolis 500 parade and ride the President's Council for Physical Fitness float with Arnold.

After it was all over, Kevin met with Dan, Fritz, and Leah and they analyzed Kevin's performance over the previous two days—especially in his relations with Arnold.

"I know I should be more careful, I know we're under the microscope now," said Kevin. "But if I'm out there doing things and saying things everyday, and I'm not hurting anybody, or trying to do wrong, and people still want to analyze what I say and do and make something out of it, then that's not my fault. If those people make you get gun-shy, that's not good, either. You gotta do what's right, you gotta be the best you can be, and you gotta treat others like you want to be treated. I make some mistakes because I'm out there doing all the time. I can't do everything perfect every time."

On Monday January 11, Kevin and the rest of the

President's Council, (except Arnold) were driven to the White House to meet with President Bush.

The council members gave President Bush accounts of their different programs, and Capt. Butterfield introduced Kevin. Butterfield commented that Arnold would probably stay on the Council—even after President Bush left office—because of his tremendous contributions to the Council.

Then, one by one, they all went to the Oval Office to get their pictures taken with the President. Arnold had told everybody ahead of time—"No schmoozing mit der President."

When Kevin's turn came, he told him that he lived in Houston and that he would love to see him when he moves there and keep him up on what's happening with the President's Council on Physical Fitness and the Americans with Disabilities Act. President Bush replied, "Yes, we will have to do that."

After the photo session, Kevin went to the offices of the President's Council on Physical Fitness where he was briefed on Council procedures.

On Tuesday, January 12, the final day of Kevin's stay in Washington D.C., he'd been invited to a luncheon honoring President Bush and Senator Dole for their work in passing the Americans with Disabilities Act.

President Bush spoke first and paid tribute to Senator Dole, saying, "He's probably the one guy in the country who has done more for people with disabilities than anyone. He deserves this more than I do."

And again, when Senator Dole spoke, he chose to spend part of his speech praising Kevin, even as the television cameras continued to roll:

"Thank you. It is a pleasure to join with you in saluting a man I am proud to call my president and friend. President George Bush and his administration will be remembered for many things: His vision in making the world a safer place for future generations, his courage in drawing the line in the sand in the Persian Gulf, his leadership in creating a new spirit of volunteerism, which has swept the nation—the list goes on and on.

"But I believe that when the history books are written, they will reflect the fact that one of his greatest accomplishments was the opportunities that were created for 43 million Americans with disabilities.

"Many of you here have heard me talk about the motto of Kansas: To the Stars Through Difficulties. And no doubt about it: countless men and women with disabilities have been able to reach their stars because of the leadership of President George Bush. Like many here in the audience, I will never forget the July day when President Bush signed the ADA into law. It was a day that simply never would have happened without the President's leadership.

"It was also his White House that gave unprecedented access and support to Americans with disabilities and it was his personal insistence that led to the appointment of more people with disabilities to more key positions than in any other administration.

"Good people like Evan Kemp, Justin Dart, Sandy Parrino, and Debbie McFadden... to name just a few. I know many of the men and women he appointed are here in the audience today. But I want to introduce you to a young man who is one of his newest appointments and who is a personal friend of mine.

"In October, President Bush appointed Kevin Saunders to serve as the first person with a disability on the President's Council on Physical Fitness.

"Paralyzed from the chest down more than a decade ago in a grain elevator explosion, Kevin has overcome adversity to become best all-around wheelchair athlete in the world, representing America in the Paralympics and in the Pan-American Games.

"Kevin was in Washington this weekend for his first meeting as a member of the President's Council, and I invited him here today so all of you could get a chance to meet this inspiring young man.

"Kevin, could you please raise your hand? When Kevin competes in competitions, the symbol of success is the gold medal. And I think it is very fitting that, beginning today, the symbol for those who seek to empower people with disabilities will be called the George Bush Medal."

"Afterwards, I told Senator Dole that that was the greatest honor anyone had ever given me," Kevin said.

Chapter 16

In the days since Kevin was named to the President's Council on Physical Fitness, his life has continued at a dizzying pace. He splits his time between motivational speaking and working on his dream of creating a wheelchair-bound action figure for the motion pictures.

In early 1993, a treatment of his life story began making the rounds in Hollywood through the powerful William Morris Agency. Kevin continued to perfect his motivational speaking through countless appearances throughout the Southwest. He also signed an agreement with the producers of the American Disabilities Channel to host a regular program featuring Americans with disabilities, entitled "Achievers." And he continued to work out, as hard as ever—or harder—with an eye of going for the gold in Atlanta in 1996.

"I'm focusing on these school presentations and improving my speaking ability," Kevin said. "But I want to do some new presentations for the kids. I'm discovering a new message, a message that says that maybe not everyone can be a world champion, a world record-holder, or a gold medalist. The idea is that you always go for the gold, do the best that you can do. And as long as you do that, you'll know inside that you've won.

"That's maybe the reason behind what happened to me in Barcelona—maybe I needed to focus more on *that* message to the kids. That's what I'm doing, I'm focusing more in that direction. My son Steven helped me realize that, that the champion is inside of everyone. Like Garth Brooks sings, some of God's greatest gifts are unanswered prayers."

Many others believe Kevin's particular gift is his ability to speak. He awes and inspires every audience he addresses.

And not just adults—he is especially adept in inspiring children. Even before he speaks in elementary schools, the children are profoundly attracted to him. They wander forward, shyly at first, then with confidence. They touch his chair, his biceps, his blonde, spiky hair. And in their midst, Kevin is continually talking in a soothing monotone, giving a moment in the sun to each and every child.

"I think something good has come out of his accident," claims Kevin's mother. "If Kevin hadn't had his accident, he would never have been going around speaking to schools, going to hospitals. Before he was hurt, he never had time to fool with young'uns or the sick. Now, he really gives them something.

"His personality has changed for the better since the accident. He's not the same person he was before. To me, he seems happier than he did before."

His parents, his friends, his coaches, even his fiercest co-competitors, all agree that something happened to Kevin in the days following Barcelona. It was a change almost on par with his change on Cardiac Hill in Atlanta.

Cardiac Hill had been a change from depression and complacency to focus and motivation. Eventually, focus became something akin to obsession. The loss of the gold medal in the Paralympics helped fuel the change from obsession back to focus.

Not that Kevin has conquered all of the demons in his life. Depression is almost always a serious problem with paraplegics and quadriplegics. As he considers life post-Barcelona, post-President's Council, it is like an ugly shadow that follows him—even on the brightest, sunniest days.

"I still have some depression," Kevin admitted, "like when I didn't win the gold medal. But I'm happy to tell kids who have been through things like I have—whether it is a terrible accident or a divorce in your family or your business fails or maybe you've lost somebody you love—that it *does* get better. It does! Given time, it... gets... better.

"Now, for the most part, I always feel great, I feel like going for it. As for my accident, I'm to the point now where I just accept it happened, then go on. The less the time you dwell on your problems or anything negative, the better off you are. You just have to focus on what you do have control over."

Kevin has said those words so many times that they are like a mantra to him. He says them with such conviction that it is like he is almost *willing* his life to conform to his words, as if he can change his circumstances through the sheer force of his will. It's a terrible burden to carry alone.

"It would be nice to have a relationship with someone now that I've cut down on my training schedule," Kevin said. "I went through a shattering time with my ex-wife and after that I had real problems with girls.

"I fell in love with a girl after my divorce, but I was always afraid that someday she'd want a guy on his feet. You just can't believe a pretty girl would want you. And you run them off. I was afraid of what *might* happen.

"Sometimes women see me in a chair and, instead of dating me as an equal, want to be my surrogate mother, to take care of me—with none of the other risks of dating involved."

So what *is* ahead for Kevin Saunders? For one thing, he says, he hopes there is a continual maturing process.

"I also think it is important that you believe in God and have a faith in God," he said. "You need to give God the glory for what you've achieved. Without Him, you wouldn't have the opportunity to reach all these goals. To be thankful to be here, to be alive and breathing, to notice the beautiful things around you, the trees, the flowers, the sunshine, your homes, your friends—all of the good things—to be thankful to God for them coming into your life, that's important. You need to be thankful for the opportunity to go out there each day and give your best to reach these goals, and reach these dreams.

"I know it is more complex than that, that there's a lot of things involved as far as how you live your life, how you go about reaching these things, or doing these things. But you don't want to make it more complex than it needs to be, either.

"It is human nature to complain, but you've got to rise above it. I'm thankful for all these things in my life. I thank God for what I have, rather than complain about what's gone."

Does he regret the eighty-hour weeks spent pumping iron and wheeling madly around paved tracks at dawn?

"My quest for the gold medal was just something that had to be done, it was a step that had to be taken, regardless of what happened in the end, or to my life along the way," Kevin said. "I don't think I missed anything because I was working toward a goal, I was trying to reach something, to get somewhere with my life. In that respect, to have done anything else I would have been going nowhere. I had a specific goal. A goal that would help me to reach other goals. And I think it was time well spent—win, lose or draw. I think everything worked perfectly.

"Maybe I'll be able to reach more people than if I had won. The more people I can identify with, the more people I can reach. There's a lot more people who identify with a guy who is almost making it than a guy who makes it all the time.

"Besides, nothing's really changed in my life, in my outlook. I tend to follow Tony Robbins' outlook on life: 'What would you do if you knew you couldn't fail?'"

In the end, Kevin is considering a host of options—continuing to compete, working on his wheelchair action figure concept, continuing his motivational speaking career, and others.

"I'd hate to leave competition because I know I could do so much better this time around," he said. "I'm leaving that open. I'm not a quitter, I never have been, and I don't plan to start now."

Judy Einbinder is among those urging him to continue in competition, at least for a few more years:

"I think that as far as he's gotten, he still got a little bit of distance to go before he reaches that final golden moment. I think he has his heart set on Atlanta, partly because it is at home. And I expect that he will do whatever it takes to get there in 1996. And because I've seen him really implement the training the last couple of years, I expect the next two years will show that. I hope he doesn't get too caught up in the movie things and promotional things and speaking things so that his training suffers for it. Because the bottom line is that you can't be the best by just talking about being the best, you've got to put the time in. And, so far, Kevin's done just that."

Kevin's second option, in some people's minds anyway, is some kind of political activism.

"The rights of the disabled is an issue I have a concern with and I want to see that progress" he said. "People in society are starting to change—to see a person with a disability as a person. To do that, you need to make things accessible in the work force and in everyday life. Whether you're shopping or working somewhere, you've got to have accessibility to the place. And you've got to know that you've got just as much right to a job as a person on their feet.

"I think the ADA is great legislation and I think it is something that's going to be a powerful, positive force in the future.

"I just don't know how far you take activism in something like this. If a place doesn't have a ramp, I don't let a little thing like a ramp stop me. I'm not a big boycotter, I don't know about standing around outside with the signs and protest stuff—that's not me. I'd rather go another route. I'd rather introduce the owner to an older lady who would like to shop there or eat there, but never could because it is not accessible. Most owners don't want to do that to a nice old lady. If not then you might mention that, by law, the owner needs to comply—if they don't want to get fined. The law itself is forcing compliance. That approach seems a more likely route for me for the future."

And finally, there is the option—or at least the dream—

of developing the action-oriented wheelchair figure. Each day, Kevin dreams and plans and schemes of ways to bring this concept to life on the big screen. He's developing a comic book based around the concept, an animated TV series, even a children's book. As a result, perhaps for the first time in his life, he's spending as much time at the drafting table and drawing board as he is in the weight-room.

"I know that if you focus, that if you put all of your energies toward something, you can be just like a powerful machine moving toward your goals," Kevin said. "My next goals are the TV-movie of my life story, and the big-screen with my action-packed wheelchair guy—as well as a cartoon character and a comic book.

"I want to bring this guy to life on the screen because I think that therein lies how we can change people's ideas about disabled people. Those preconceptions can be changed. And television and film are the most powerful media in the world."

And what if Kevin fails? What if Hollywood never embraces the idea of a physically challenged hero?

"Fear is the biggest killer of dreams you can have," Kevin said. "If your mind is on winning, that's what you'll do."

So, in the end, does Kevin ever know fear? It's hard to be afraid of failure when you've survived a shattered skull, collapsed lungs, and a severed spine. But that's not to say he never knows fear. When he drives north on Highway 37 from his comfortable, wheelchair-accessible house, he can't help but look at the Public Grain Elevator, a giant concrete monolith that dominates the landscape by the Corpus Christi ship channel.

And when he sees it, he can't help but remember.

Does Kevin ever know fear? Perhaps one time he did, ironically just a few weeks after the Games in Barcelona.

On the night of November 8, 1992, Kevin and Kent Oliver were awakened by a bone-rattling rumble, followed by a thunderous boom. The shock waves that followed tumbled the two from their respective beds.

As they looked out of the windows facing Highway 37,

the house was suddenly filled with a piercing brightness, a light so bright it hurt to look into it. Directly across the highway was a landscape out of hell. Flames leaped above the telephone poles and electric power lines. Even across 37, the heat was so intense that the walls and windows of the house facing that direction were hot to the touch.

Dan was the only witness.

"I happened to be sitting on the couch, which was the perfect view," he said. "I couldn't go to sleep and I was watching TV. I looked to the left because I heard the initial boom and the whole picture window was completely covered in a ball of flame.

"It was insane, I'd never seen anything like it in my life.

"That was immediately following the flash, and a two to three hundred foot-wide, hundred foot-high flame just came billowing up out of the ground."

What the three friends were seeing was liquid petroleum gas, which is transported via underground pipes at three hundred degrees below zero. Liquid petroleum gas is incredibly explosive. And because the pipes are so cold that they freeze the ground around them, the pipes are usually buried eight feet underground.

Somehow, a pipeline elbow had broken and the gas had leaked out and eventually ignited.

Dan and Kent were trying to awaken and evacuate their neighbors as the flames billowed higher and higher. But, perhaps for the first time since the grain elevator explosion, Kevin felt the icy claw of panic.

"For a moment, it scared the hell out of me," Kevin said, "I thought we were all goners. It looked like a nuclear explosion. I could see what had happened to me happening to Dan and Kent. And I couldn't stand the thought. I thought the whole Citco Refinery was going up because two hundred feet from that flame were billions of gallons of fuel. I couldn't move, all I could remember was that rumble more than twelve years ago."

Dan finally convinced Kevin and Kent to leave and he remained to take photographs for the Corpus Christi newspaper.

Fortunately, the pipeline's built-in dampers kept the fire from spreading, though the highway was shut down for more than four hours.

Kevin returned home an hour later, the initial wave of fear and adrenaline long gone. He sat for long moments watching the fire. Dan asked him why he'd returned so quickly.

"You can't live your life scared," Kevin said, "you've got to face your fears. More than the fire, the rumbling before the explosion was my fear. Sometimes I hear it in my sleep and I wake up and the first thing I check are my legs. Can I move my legs? Sometimes I dream I'm running and I run for hours to nowhere in particular.

"Once I left the house, I realized that this was just a little flame. I'd already been purified by a much bigger flame, a flame and explosion that were a hundred times bigger than this one. This was just a little reminder to me of where I'd been, what I'd been through. It reminded me that I'd made it."

According to Dan, Kevin then calmly returned to bed and slept through several hours of firetrucks and police sirens wailing, men shouting orders, and the booming roar of the runaway fire just across the highway.

Tomorrow would be a busy day and Kevin decided he needed his sleep. There were miles to run, weights to pump, letters to write, speeches to give, movies to make, shows to host.

A life to live.

Because there's always a way.